LILY TOMLIN

LILY

TOMLIN

WOMAN OF A THOUSAND FACES

JEFF SORENSEN

ST. MARTIN'S PRESS—NEW YORK

Design by Jaye Zimet

Library of Congress Cataloging-in-Publication Data
Sorensen, Jeff.
    Lily Tomlin: woman of a thousand faces / Jeff Sorensen.
        p.   cm.
    ISBN 0-312-03386-9
    1. Tomlin, Lily. 2. Comedians—United States—Biography.
    3. Motion picture actors and actresses—United States—Biography.
    I. Title.
    PN2287.T64S67   1989
    792.7′028′092—dc20
    [B]   89-35117

First Edition

10 9 8 7 6 5 4 3 2 1

CONTENTS

1 Lily Tomlin's Gallery of Characters 1

2 "She Was a Free Spirit" 11

3 Improvisations 25

4 "One Ringy-Dingy . . ." 41

5 This Is a Recording 57

6 Modern Screen 77

7 Appearing Nitely 93

8 A Moment to Forget 107

9 Lily Tomlin—Movie Star 119

10 Signs of Intelligent Life on Broadway 153

11 Big Business 177

12 A Real Perfectionist 191

INDEX 198

LILY TOMLIN

CHAPTER 1

LILY TOMLIN'S GALLERY OF CHARACTERS

Her voice is as dainty as a burglar alarm. Her face is set in a perpetual grimace, somehow managing to smile and snarl at the same time. Every muscle in her body seems completely tense. While she talks, she is liable to move around in her seat like a hyperactive child. When she finishes a sentence, she usually sticks out her tongue a little and emits a gleeful snort.

"One ringy-dingy. Two ringy-dingys. A gracious good afternoon to you," she will typically say at the beginning of one of her telephone conversations. "Have I reached the party to whom I am speaking?" And if the party to whom she is speaking says something ungracious, she will probably show her irritation by responding, "You are not talking with just anyone's fool . . . I am a high school graduate."

No fan of Lily Tomlin's needs to be told that this is a description of Ernestine, the telephone operator. Anyone who has ever worked in an office can recognize her as a type we're all familiar with: a low-level employee who enjoys exercising the tiny bit of power she has over other people, especially the customers. In fact, Ernestine gets a kind of sexual thrill out of mercilessly putting the screws on people who are behind in paying their phone bills. One of Tomlin's best-known routines is Ernestine's telephone encounter with Gore Vidal, whom she takes special pleasure in harassing and whose name she mispronounces:

"Mr. Veedle, you owe us a balance of $23.64. When may we expect payment? . . . Pardon? When *what* freezes over? . . . I don't see why you're kicking up such a ruckus when according to our files your present bank balance, plus stocks, securities, and other holdings, amounts to exactly . . . Pardon? . . . Privileged information? Oh! (snort, snort) Mr. Veedle, that's so cute! No, no, no, you're dealing with the telephone company. We are not subject to city, state, or federal legislation. We are omnipotent." When Vidal still refuses to knuckle under, Ernestine tells him she may be forced to release some of the recordings of his calls, which the phone company has been making for years. "I think blackmail is such an ugly word," says Ernestine. "Let's just call it a vicious threat."

Poignantly frustrated Ernestine, who was first introduced to us on "Rowan and Martin's Laugh-In," is just one member of the gallery of characters created by Lily Tomlin. There are dozens more—a tribute to Tomlin's chameleon-like ability to remake herself into practically anyone she wishes. She accomplishes these transformations with breathtaking ease, not even requiring changes of costume or makeup. Her kaleidoscopic face and her extraordinarily expressive gestures are all that she really needs onstage.

This gift is what has made Tomlin one of America's favorite comediennes over the past twenty years. She's been in hit movies, such as *9 to 5* (1980) and *All of Me* (1984), has released several popular and critically acclaimed comedy record albums, has won five Emmies for her TV specials—and has brought her one-woman theater troupe to Broadway in such plays as *Appearing Nitely* and *The Search for Signs of Intelligent Life in the Universe.* Moreover, she is usually not only the performer but one of the writers of her material.

Lily seems to have a particular fondness for eccentric characters and for down-and-out types of people: She specializes in the forgotten, unglamorous, lost souls who would never be interviewed on "Lifestyles of the Rich and Famous." And she has observed these people so perceptively that we immediately recognize them from our own experiences.

One of the most memorable of these is Trudy, the shopping bag lady. She may be "certifiably" crazy, but she is in the habit of saying things that make a certain amount of sense. For example: "You'd think by now evolution could've at least evolved us to the point where we could change ourselves." Or: "I can take reality in small doses, but as a lifestyle I found it too confining." Or: "Goin' crazy was the best thing ever happened to me. I don't say it's for everybody; some people couldn't cope."

It's clear that Tomlin relishes every moment of her portrayal of Trudy, who is an especially colorful character. Trudy walks with a pronounced stoop, her voice is less than mellifluous, and she has a habit of squinting so much that her eyes are like half-moons.

She is a woman of a type whom we have all seen on city street corners: in real life, we might find ourselves edging away from her, but onstage she is endearing. An important part of her appeal is that she feels free, because she's a social outcast, to say lots of things that we may sometimes feel but don't want to admit to anyone else.

Another engaging Tomlin impersonation is Agnus Angst, a teenage punkster who says that she and her grandparents "have nothing in common except that we are all carbon-based life forms." "When I look at my family," she says, "I feel like a detached retina." As her name indicates, Agnus isn't particularly happy about her situation; she is trying to use G. Gordon Liddy's book *Will* as a self-help guide. Her motto seems to be: "I'm getting my act together, throwing it in your face. I want to insult every member of the human race."

Edith Ann is a little demon of a five-year-old who claims, "I don't usually get a cold. I have leprosy." Like other girls, she enjoys playing with dolls—but in her own way. She stuffs the dolls under her dress and pretends to be pregnant.

Mrs. Beasley, on the other hand, puts all of her energies into becoming the "perfect" housewife. In one routine Mrs. Beasley endorses a sexual aid called Good Vibrations, which she describes as "a kind of Hamburger Helper for the boudoir."

The list of Tomlin impersonations goes on and on. Kate, a rich woman who suffers from "affluenza," says, "A bored species connot survive." Lyn is a disillusioned feminist, who has come to the conclusion that, "If I had known what it would be like to have it all . . . I might have settled for less." Another character is called The Cheerleader, and Tomlin describes her as "one who does for enthusiasm what Muzak does for music."

And then there's Glenna, "a child of the sixties." Tomlin shows how Glenna reacts to every sixties fad. In one sketch, Glenna is upset to hear that, "Meg says that Paul's dead; he's the only one barefoot on the *Abbey Road* album. She says if you play 'I Am the Walrus' backwards you can hear them saying 'Paul is dead.' But so is Malcolm. And Bobby and Martin Luther King . . . or maybe it's the other way around. I can't even remember who was assassinated in order anymore, can you?"

Tomlin does a great scalpel job on some typical sixties attitudes when she portrays Glenna. After Glenna takes LSD, she describes how "I came to this, like, cosmic understanding of a Lipton flow-through tea bag." On another occasion she tells a friend, "I met the most beautiful white dude in my black studies class."

The key to the success of Tomlin's portrayals is that she sympathizes with all of these people. We never get the sense that she feels she is superior to her characters: Tomlin manages to find something in common with even the oddest of the lot.

As she comments, "I don't necessarily admire them, but I do them all with love. After all, in private we're all misfits."

Her longtime collaborator, Jane Wagner, says, "Lily is after something beyond formulas—not sketches, not naturalism, not black comedy. Call it maybe docu-comedy, something that reveals human nature—absurd, touching, grotesque, and overwhelming."

Lily's enthusiasm for her work is obvious to even the most nearsighted member of her audience. She loves to perform, and she slips from one role to another with the ease—and the delight—of a child rummaging through a trunkful of old clothes and trying on whatever happens to strike her fancy. Although acting is her profession, we never get the sense that she regards her performances as merely "a job." She says, "I really feel I *am* those people I play." And because she believes in them so intensely, we believe in them as well.

Tomlin is not the sort of performer who has been able to learn much about acting from classrooms. She feels that if she tried to analyze what she does, she might be unable to continue doing it naturally. "Years ago when I started out," Tomlin remembers, "I tried to go to acting classes. I'd get so confused when I tried to do what I thought I'd been learning . . . I'd get such strange criticism that I couldn't even understand it, and when I'd feel humiliated to the last inch, I'd chuck the learning and resort to something instinctive. I wanted to study, but I couldn't make much headway."

Her approach has always been based on closely observing real people, rather than watching other performers. As a result her style of acting is quite different from most contemporary actors and actresses.

"Creating characters has a great appeal for me," says Lily. "It is a process I invented to give me something to do. This is what captured me when I decided I wanted to become a performer. I can be in the neighborhood store where I live, suddenly picking up the antics or body style of a man in a phone booth having an animated conversation with someone miles away. Or it could be the street people and their strange, sometimes ritualistic behavior and movement.''

Many of her best characterizations are based on the people Lily knew when she was growing up in Detroit. "We lived in an old apartment house and I was exposed to a huge range of people," she says. "The building itself was a real microcosm, and I was an independent kid who could visit from one apartment to the next, adapt to the different people, and totally enjoy myself.''

Very often, Lily talks about her characters in a way that sounds almost schizophrenic. When she turned down $500,000 from AT&T to portray Ernestine in a commercial, Lily told one reporter, "Oh no, she wouldn't do that." On another occasion Lily said, "Do you think Ernestine is not a real person? Do you think my characters are not real? They're out there somewhere. I just imitate them.''

George Schlatter, who was the executive producer of "Rowan and Martin's Laugh-In," comments, "Lily doesn't just do her characters, she becomes them. She can describe Edith Ann's room to you. She can tell you about Ernestine's sex life. Lily is an actress who happens to be a comic.''

But she isn't strictly naturalistic in her approach to acting; after all, audiences wouldn't be entertained by characters who aren't a little larger than they are in real life. "My comedy is actual life with the slightest twist of exaggeration," explains Lily. "I construct compressed accuracy, a character essence that is as true and real as I can get it. I don't go for laughter. I never play for a joke per se. If the joke gets in the character's way, I take it out."

This dedication to her characters is at the heart of Tomlin's appeal. She tends to become obsessed with getting every detail of her performance just right, almost as if she would be somehow letting her characters down if she didn't do them full justice. Very few other actresses bring the same amount of intensity to her work that Tomlin does. And not too surprisingly, those who have worked with her say she can often become a bit exasperating in her demands that everyone live up to her own high standards. Even Tomlin doesn't dispute that she is a full-blown workaholic. When asked if she ever takes a day off, she says she has trouble remembering her last one.

Essentially, Tomlin is a lively and determined woman who has chosen to devote nearly all of her energy to the creation of characters who seem believable to the audience. She has a craving for versatility, and has, unlike so many other performers, kept challenging herself to do new parts that stretch the limits of her abilities. Time and time again she has succeeded in differentiating each new character from the old, right down to the nuances of Trudy's jagged smile or Ernestine's cackling laugh.

Of course, it takes more than just hard work for Tomlin to accomplish what she does. She is also gifted with a good ear for the rhythms of everyday speech and a real flair for imitating people. She has a face like Silly Putty that can be molded into whatever expression she may need for a particular character. (Photographs of Lily often look amazingly different— sometimes it's hard to believe they are all of the same person.) Not many other actors or actresses are as skilled as she at mimicking voices; Peter Sellers may have been one of the few who could compete with her in this area.

Tomlin has always expressed her social and political points of view in her work. Although there are rarely any explicit messages in her comedy routines, it's plain to any attentive observer that she holds a number of strong convictions. For instance, she won't perform material that she feels is demeaning toward women. She also often takes aim at big targets such as the FBI, the phone company, and IBM, and has never been afraid of confrontations with powerful producers and network executives over her material. Her TV specials from the early seventies, in particular, were much more daring than most of what was being broadcast at that time.

Tomlin's routines were important influences on recent TV comedy programs such as "Saturday Night Live" and "SCTV." In fact, Lorne Michaels, who was one of the producers of Tomlin's early specials, later became the producer of "Saturday Night Live." He explains, "There was an air of being subversive about what she was doing back then." He credits Lily Tomlin's work as one of the main inspirations for "Saturday Night Live." He was especially impressed by her willingness to expand the boundaries of what was considered "acceptable" material for television. "She's always been the bravest woman I know," he says.

What led her to be more daring than other TV comics, it seems clear, is the very same dedication to her characters that makes her performances seem so vital and credible. As Michaels comments, "Once she created a reality, she would never betray it."

CHAPTER 2

"SHE WAS
A FREE
SPIRIT"

Lily Tomlin is most herself when she's being someone else. From a very early age, she discovered that she enjoyed watching people and imitating how they behaved. In her imagination she *became* them. She had a rich fantasy life, partly because her real life wasn't always a pleasant one. As a performer, Lily has been able to take what often was a painful childhood and turn it into the basis of her comedy. "I don't know if humor is a compensation for pain," she says, "but if it is, it doesn't seem like a bad one."

Of all her characters, "Probably the closest to the real me is Edith Ann. . . . I was such a smart-alecky child," explains Lily.

Independent-minded as a youngster, she was in the habit of doing precisely whatever she wanted. Even her mother, Lillie Mae Tomlin, admits that "Lily was always a stubborn child, and I went along with a lot of things that other mothers didn't."

Lily was born in Detroit on September 1, 1939,

and was christened Mary Jean Tomlin. (She didn't start calling herself Lily until she got into show business in the mid-sixties.) Her parents, Guy and Lillie Mae, were from Paducah, Kentucky, and many of Lily's relatives still live there. Quite a few of Lily's characters in her comedy routines, such as Mrs. Beasley, speak with Kentucky accents. In fact, Lily herself will occasionally speak with a distinctly Southern twang, especially when she's in an upbeat, talkative mood.

The Tomlin family had recently moved from Kentucky, where jobs were scarce during the Depression, to Detroit, where Guy found work as a toolmaker with the Commonwealth Brass Company. Guy took a considerable amount of pride in his work, Lily recalls. He would sometimes bring parts home from the factory and give them to his daughter, saying, "Look at these, Babe, this is what Papa did today." He also gave her some advice that she would never forget: "Babe, pay no attention to what other people think. Just be yourself."

Though he worked hard, Lily remembers that her father was "a drinking man and a gambling man." He sometimes lost a week's wages during visits to the racetrack, often at times when the family badly needed the money. He was completely unconventional and unpredictable. "He was the type of man," explains Lily, "who when the Jehovah's Witnesses lady came to the door, he'd say, 'Come on in. I'm about to have a Miller High Life—how about you?'"

"My parents were crazy, wonderful, individual Southern eccentrics," says Lily. But it was a household apparently full of conflicts: while her mother craved respectability, her father was contemptuous of it. "He met my mother, Lillian Ford, this very bright, very witty woman, and a sweet, pretty lady bent—oh my yes—on middle-class respectability." Lily's comedy sketches about Lud and Marie are fond evocations of Guy and Lillie Mae Tomlin.

The other member of the Tomlin family was Richard, Lily's brother, who is four years younger than she. (Richard now works as an interior designer.) Lillie Mae and Guy found their children to be unusually willful youngsters. By the time Lily and Richard were old enough to go to school, they were pretty much allowed to do what they liked. "We never behaved too well," remembers Lily. "We were never subjected to the parent-child relationship, either because we saw through our parents, or they just didn't fit the roles well. And we understood early on that our parents didn't know everything. Like, they couldn't make us go to bed, so finally they stopped trying. . . . My parents would go to bed, and Richard and I would stay up until two in the morning. Richard would put on a satin smoking jacket, light a cigarette, and march around with a glass of something. I really think Mother sensed that we might take a stick to her if she didn't stop telling us what to do. So she decided to stop mothering."

Lily and Richard overheard the arguments that their parents frequently had about money and about Guy's gambling and drinking. "Problems weren't hidden from us," Lily says. "We learned a lot about life at an early age. There are millions of kids in middle-class, suburban neighborhoods who never know that people need money or where it comes from, or if their mothers and fathers fight. We knew it all."

The Tomlins' neighborhood in Detroit was far from well-to-do. According to Lily, "Success in my neighborhood meant, if you were a girl, not getting pregnant; if you were a boy, not going to jail. Everything else was okey-dokey."

The neighborhood was changing rapidly during Lily's childhood. She explains, "We were working class, but we were surrounded by people of all types, and there was constant drama unfolding. It was a little working-class ghetto just outside a very affluent neighborhood. All of our neighbors were either on their way up or on their way down."

Until she was fifteen, recalls Lily, "We lived on Hazelwood, between Byron and Woodrow Wilson. We lived in the D'Elce Apartments . . . within six or seven blocks of the D'Elce were Boston and Chicago Boulevards. There were incredible, three-hundred-thousand-dollar houses on those streets. To the north was Sherwood Forest, where the rich Jews lived, and farther north were the rich Gentiles, who were running away from the Jews, right? When I was four or five, the first blacks moved to Hazelwood. Now it's all black where I grew up, and the whole neighborhood burned down in the riots in 1967."

Lily says there were "some really beautiful people at the D'Elce. I was one of those kids who would go around to everybody's apartment and hang out. I just loved it because there were so many classes of people. I could go to the guy who was a radical Communist in the building, and he was always giving me propaganda books to read. And then I would go over to see Mrs. Rupert, who was a real conservative, a real reactionary, and very eccentric."

Lily was especially enthralled by Mrs. Rupert. She was such a delightful character that Lily began spending most of her free time with her. "I came to realize that she was the first great eccentric I'd known at close range," Lily says. Mrs. Rupert emptied the garbage wearing fox furs. She was a botanist, and she kept her windows sealed up so that her apartment would be more like a greenhouse. She told Lily that both of her sons were in the CIA—and Lily believed her without question. Eventually Mrs. Rupert decided to take Lily in hand and tutor her in the ways of the world.

"She told me she was going to teach me how to raise myself above my fated station in life," Lily says. "I began a long relationship with her. Our daily ritual began as soon as I got through with dinner at home and went downstairs to walk Chico and Sonny, Mrs. Rupert's chihuahuas, for which I was paid fifteen cents. Then we'd read *The New York Times* from cover to cover. I'd have to look up words I'd never heard before in the dictionary while she did the crossword puzzle. And every Saturday, she'd take me shopping with her. We'd go to places like Hudson's, the big Detroit department store. She showed me how to select and care for linens, silver, and all the equipment necessary to be a lady . . . and she tried to teach me how to organize my pocketbook. 'A lady,' she'd say, 'is never supposed to rummage in her purse.'"

Although Lily was a lively girl who enjoyed being at the center of attention, and who liked to make people laugh, she didn't dream that one day she would be a famous performer. Becoming a movie star, she says, never entered her mind. "My neighbors were far more interesting to me than Rita Hayworth or Lana Turner. If I went to the movies at all as a child, it was to torment people—throw candy, and run up and down the aisles with my friends. I just didn't relate to show business. It seemed so unreal in terms of the kind of life I lived."

As a young girl she was receiving the most important part of her education from her observations of the people she knew. She wasn't all that interested in her classes at Crossman Elementary and Hutchins Junior High schools. Yet she was naturally bright, enough so that she got above-average grades most of the time.

Early on, she learned the importance of having her own income. She saw that working at a job gave her more independence, and it was her desire to be as independent as she could possibly be.

When she was seven, she remembers sending away for "a whole bunch of old sleazy stuff advertised in the back of a comic book, like itching powder and hand buzzers. It came C.O.D. and cost eleven dollars. My poor mother was intimidated enough to pay for it, but when I got home from school, she said, 'You can't have it until you can pay me back.' I said, 'How's a kid supposed to get any money?' 'You could,' she answered, 'do errands for people.' That was a revelation to me. I don't know why I hadn't thought of it myself. There were about forty apartments in our building, and so I sent around a list of things I would do—like go to the store or take down the garbage for ten cents. From then on I had the money to buy what I wanted, or I could chip in the extra two dollars to buy a more glamorous pair of shoes." As soon as she reached the legal working age—which was fourteen—she began applying for jobs outside the building. During the next few years she worked as a receptionist at a chiropractor's office and as a clerk at several stores in Detroit.

Her classmates from Cass Technical High School remember Lily, whom they knew only as Mary Jean, as a very popular young woman. Mary Jean/Lily was quick-witted and quick-moving, and she had bright eyes and a high-voltage smile. She was a pretty, long-legged girl who was extremely energetic.

Sharon Scanlan Ballios was a member of the class of 1957, along with Lily, and they were both cheerleaders for Cass Tech. Ballios says, "Her first stage experience—Mary Jean's first experience with the thrill of being in front of an audience—was when she was a cheerleader. She wasn't in any plays in high school, so cheerleading was the theater for her at that time. Cass Tech was a big school and the auditorium was four floors high. When we had a pep rally it was almost like being on Broadway."

Lily describes herself as "the best white cheerleader Detroit ever had," and Sharon Ballios says, "Mary Jean was very enthusiastic about cheerleading. She was athletic and limber, very acrobatic. She was like a rubber band, almost. I think she learned a lot about cheerleading from watching the black students and the way they cheered. You know we all learned how to dance in the fifties from copying the black styles. There was a dance called The Chicken, which was popular then, and it was started by the blacks. I remember that Lily really enjoyed doing The Chicken."

Ballios feels that becoming a cheerleader was even more important for Lily than for the others on the squad. "Her family was very poor; they were sort of borderline hillbillies, even. So to be selected as a cheerleader was really something special for her. When you come from that background and you get to be a cheerleader, which means being recognized as very popular with your classmates, it is a real self-esteem boost. And underneath, Mary Jean always had a little insecurity—even now I think you can sense that. But being a cheerleader certainly helped her."

Like every teenager, Lily had some insecurities about her appearance. She remembers putting on a bathing suit and lying down next to a mirror in order to study her reflection. "What I wanted, more than anything else, was that Esther Williams full roundness in my hips. Mine were flat. That bit I do about putting padding in my hips when I was a high school cheerleader—absolutely true."

Ballios says Lily had a reputation for being "kind of a little devil. She was mildly rebellious, though not really rebellious at all by today's standards. . . . I remember that our school band once went off to Chicago for a competition, and Mary Jean wanted to see them play; so she just decided to hitchhike there, all by herself. She was gone from school for a few days before they caught her and sent her back on a bus.

"A few of us girls, including Mary Jean, formed a sorority, which was supposed to be illegal at our school. It was called Epsilon Ni Omega. I still have the old sweatshirts that we wore. They were a horrible shade of purple; I don't know why we picked out that color. On the sweatshirts there was a cross, a star of David, a branch, and a sun. And we had a little sorority cottage for a while, where we just had a riot."

Lily says she went through a "semi-hood stage" around this time. She smoked Pall Malls, and "I looked like something off the cover of *True Confessions*." The girls in the sorority wore "lots of black" and red angel decals on their dresses, recalls Lily.

Another member of the Class of '57 at Cass Tech, Janet Davis Hughes, explains, "She was a free spirit. She liked to do funny, creative things. One time Mary Jean brought her mother's house dress to the cottage and some long underwear that she wore underneath. And we all went into the small town in the suburbs where the cottage was. We would go into a grocery store and she would speak in a Southern accent and pretend that we were all her children. The funny part of it was that nobody paid any attention to us, which we thought was just hysterical.

"I remember another day when she wrapped an old army blanket around herself and, in her bare feet, went chanting down the street as if she were in a trance, like some Maharishi. She'd go up to plate-glass windows and press her nose against the glass and chant at the people inside. She was always pretending to be somebody else, and was not in the least inhibited. She wasn't real reliable, but she was so much fun you could forgive her for a lot of things. Plus, she was bright enough and articulate enough to talk her way out of any trouble she might get into.

"I don't know if she ever consciously thought in high school about going into show business," Hughes says, "but I know she would never have been content to have an ordinary, humdrum life. . . . Nothing she could ever do would surprise me. Of course, we wouldn't have *expected* her to become so famous and everything later on—but when it all happened it didn't really surprise us. She was never ordinary."

After high school, Lily entered Wayne State University in Detroit as a premedical student, "Because I always had an inclination toward biology—and besides, I'm a Virgo and most of them are hypochondriacs. Seriously, though, I did envision becoming a doctor. . . . What I really wanted was to have autonomy. In those years you either had to be exceptional or be married. I never wanted to be dependent on anybody, and I was darned good in science."

But after a couple of semesters at Wayne State, she found herself unable to muster up much enthusiasm for her science and math classes. She wasn't able to breeze through college without making an effort, as she had been able to do in high school. "I was not a great student at Wayne State. I had, what do you call it, narcolepsy—I'd go home at three to study, fall asleep, and wake up at nine the next morning."

In her second year of college, Lily auditioned for a small role in a production of *The Madwoman of Chaillot*. She improvised a few moves on the spot and made a favorable impression on the director.

"In *The Madwoman* her part was really just a walk-on," recalls Margaret Spear, who was teaching in the theater department at Wayne State at that time. Spear says, "I directed her in her second play, which was *The School for Wives* by Molière; this was her first substantial part. Lily played a comic maid. Typically, the maids in Molière are very clever and outsmart their masters. The servants are the ones who help the young lovers so that everything turns out all right at the end."

Lily auditioned for Margaret Spear, who remembers: "The minute I saw her I decided to use her in *The School for Wives.* You could tell immediately that she had a sense for comedy. She didn't have much experience then, but she had what you can't teach—a sense of timing and a lot of imagination. And vitality, she still has that. Also, inventiveness. When it came to rehearsals, she and the young man who was playing the male servant would go offstage and work out little bits of business together. She was so inventive, in fact, that it became a matter of my having to cut things out and select what we could use. She had so many ideas that you just couldn't use everything she came up with, because it wouldn't have been appropriate for the play. It might have bothered many people, to have half of what they wanted to do cut out, but it didn't faze her at all. Or deter her from continuing to come up with more suggestions."

"These were the only roles she did for the theater department," says Spear, "but she was also in some plays in the studio theater. Those were shows that were directed by the students rather than the teachers. For the studio theater she did Edward Albee's *The*

Sandbox, and I remember she was wonderfully good in that. Don't forget, she was not a theater major, so these were all extracurricular activities for her."

Spear comments that Lily's attitude toward acting was apparently quite different from her attitude toward her classes. "Some people may say she was a bit of a rebel in those days, but in the theater I didn't see that side of her at all. Matter of fact, she seemed very quiet and cooperative. Away from my sight, she may have been quite different. Or it could be that I saw her in the one thing she truly was serious about."

Carol Minsky, a student from Lily's class at Wayne State, recalls that Lily became pretty well known on campus for her theatrical efforts. "But even though she was an actress, she was not a tortured soul who couldn't get along with people—the way some performers are. She was somebody who made people feel good to be with her. I remember, too, that she had so much energy that it almost exhausted you to be around her for very long at a stretch. Her wheels were always spinning on overdrive."

Another important role for Lily was in a sketch for a student variety show at Wayne State. In fact, she says that show marked "the real birth of Lily Tomlin." At first she was only given a little part to do in one sketch. "Then one day I decided to assert myself. . . . The show was short; they needed more material. I had always been able to do a takeoff on the Grosse Pointe matrons—you know, Grosse Pointe is a very rich suburb of Detroit—so I grabbed one of the actors and said, 'Let's improvise an interview. I'll be this Tasteful Lady. You ask me about my charitable activities; we'll just ad-lib things.' That was the first character I did and it was a huge success in that little college show."

As her flair for playing funny women became more apparent to Lily and her theatrical friends at Wayne State, she says that "Not only did I revel in the attention, but I also thought, 'Gee, it would be great if I could make a living doing this. I wouldn't have to finish college and get a regular job.'"

After her junior year at Wayne State, she decided to drop out of school and pursue a theatrical career. Not one for playing it safe by starting out closer to home, she chose to leave Detroit and move to New York.

CHAPTER 3

IMPROVISATIONS

Lily's first stay in New York City, in 1960, proved to be a short one. She took some mime and acting classes but soon reached the conclusion that she wasn't yet ready for the Big Time (and vice versa): "I saw people [in New York] who were so dedicated and so involved, and it was a whole other life. . . . They subjugated themselves to their art and I knew it wasn't for me, then."

Unable to find any jobs in the theater, Lily worked as an assistant bookkeeper. Her salary was eighty dollars a week, which was barely enough for her to afford a tiny apartment in the East Village. Usually, she would wear the same suit to work day after day, re-ironing it every morning. "I made a list, in this raggedy little notebook, of things I desperately wanted. To get up in the morning and have something to wear. To have a hairdo I could take care of easily, and hands that were well groomed. To have something to eat in the house when I wanted it."

A big part of Lily's problem at the time was that she didn't know much about the practical details of how to go about becoming an actress. She didn't know how to get an agent, or how to get the right kind of photographs, or which auditions were worth pursuing. "Admittedly, I should've asked around more to find out about that kind of stuff, but the problem was that I was becoming extremely discouraged." Furthermore, most of her friends in the Village weren't all that helpful: "I was living in male-dominated Bohemia—the men were painters and sculptors, and the women did the cooking and rolled the joints."

So after a few disappointing months in New York, she went back to Detroit, where she lived for the next four years. During the days she usually worked as an office temporary, and during the evenings she began to appear at small coffeehouses and cabarets. It was in this period in the early sixties that Lily began to create several of the comic characters who would later make her well known.

Her favorite Detroit night spot was a place called The Unstabled. "That's where I got myself together. We did contemporary plays, and after the theater we would do sketches and improvisations. And we had a folk singer; it was the whole coffeehouse routine. I was the only one from there who stuck it out. I stayed there for a couple of years developing material. For example, I came up with Lupe, the world's oldest beauty expert, way back then."

Russell Smith, who is now the head of design for the theater department at Wayne State, remembers

seeing Lily frequently at The Unstabled and other coffeehouses in Detroit. "There were lots of little cabarets
and theaters opening in Detroit then. But they didn't
stay around for very long. I think it was the usual
problem, where everyone was thinking about the
show and nobody was taking care of *business*. So
they couldn't stay in business very long. Anyway,
I remember that Lily's work back at that time was a
lot rougher-edged than what we all know from her
today. She wasn't nearly as professional and smooth.
Plus, she was young and still developing her style.
Some of the material she was doing was written by
her, but she would also do the revue stuff which was
written by other people—she would do crossovers
and one-liners, and whatever else was part of the
show. And she could improvise on any subject that
came up.

"In her act she was already doing the Tasteful
Lady from Grosse Pointe, with her little pillbox hat
and her gloves, who turned up later on 'Laugh-In.'
And I also remember her doing this little girl, who
was sort of like her Edith Ann character. The joke was
that the girl would start out talking very sweetly about
her 'tiny little dolly.' At the beginning you think she's
very nice, but later you realize she's actually very
nasty. At the end she becomes quite the villainess,
and she's ripping the eyes out of the dolly. As I remember, this bit was done as some kind of a song, not
just a regular monologue."

Smith was part of Lily's circle of friends in the
late fifties when she was at Wayne State and in the
early sixties when she was playing at the coffee-

houses. He recalls that although it was clear to everyone that she had an extraordinary ability to mimic people and create characters, most of those who knew her then didn't quite know what to make of her theatrical talents, which didn't fit into the usual mold. "Her success, in a way, was a surprise to many of us," says Smith. "She amused us all very much, but we tended to think it was a terribly esoteric kind of talent and she'd never get anywhere with it. So much for our intuition!

"Lily was an imaginative, creative person who was very funny and well-liked—but she didn't seem to be an actress for the theater, in the traditional sense. She wasn't interested in doing the standard repertoire of plays. She just wanted to do her own type of thing. And she didn't take any acting classes at all; she was totally self-taught. She saw the theater as a place for fun. For her, it was playing dress-up games for fun. I don't believe she felt at that time that the theater was something she *had* to do; instead, it was just something she liked to do."

Even though it was fun for Lily, she took her performances very seriously, Smith explains. "She would labor over something till the last dog had died. She enjoyed acting, yet she did have that perfectionist streak. But I think she was a little looser and more spontaneous then than she is now. She didn't try to get everything worked out down to the letter the way she does today in *The Search*."

Smith recalls that Lily was "just crazy about Ruth Draper, who was a big influence on her." Draper was a monologuist who was noted for her character sketches

and one-woman shows. Much like Lily, Draper created her own characters and was able to bring them to
life onstage without special props or costumes. She
died in 1956, but she made some records, which have
helped to keep her reputation alive. Although Draper
was never popular with a mass audience, she had a
small and devoted following, especially among those
who love the theater.

Lily never saw Draper, but when she was working
at The Unstabled, "A man told me I reminded him of
her, and I went to the library and listened to her records. . . . I responded to her because she did women
and because she did them with humanity."

In 1964, Lily returned to New York. She felt she
was now ready to become a professional comedienne,
and this time she was fully determined to persevere.
At first her engagements were mainly limited to brief
performances at the Improvisation nightclub on the
West Side of Manhattan and the Café Au Go-Go in
Greenwich Village.

Lily was definitely paying her dues during those
years. She flunked her share of auditions, played
sometimes to indifferent audiences, and remembers
"sitting morosely in a delicatessen and listening to
people talk about 'that awful girl' they had just seen
performing." To survive, Lily explains, "You have to
be insulated and believe in yourself. Anybody who
carves a little place for herself has to." She took solace
from the fact that there seemed to be few other people
doing her kind of comedy. "There didn't seem to be
any women around who were doing perceptive

humor. Most of the comediennes were doing broader stuff; they were too wacky for my taste."

Lily has never taken an interest in telling the standard jokes that most comedians do. "When I see a stand-up comic telling mother-in-law jokes," she says, "I'd rather be the mother-in-law than the comic." Another problem with the usual stand-up routines, she realized, was that the material was completely interchangeable. Any other comic could steal a joke, and it would be difficult to prove who had done it first. On the other hand, no one could steal one of her characterizations, since the humor usually came more out of her performance than out of the particular lines she said.

What's more, "When I first started out in New York I would go to the Improv and I would see lots of comedy performers who were just brilliant, wonderful. But they would never create material for themselves. I was always making up monologues, and I would go to the Improv at three in the morning and work on them. To me these other people were just as capable as I of doing that. I'd see them do some brilliant improvisation, and I'd say, 'You must record that and build a piece of material on it so that you can re-create it, do it again, refine it, and build a body of material.' It always seemed so obvious and natural to me. As a result, I accumulated and accumulated. It was just my inclination."

Silver Friedman, the owner of the Improv, remembers, "Lily came in a few times a week at that point. This was from 1964 to '66. . . . The Improv was a place where she could practice and do her thing, make mistakes, and act silly. There wasn't much pressure; it was like a house party. There were no auditions. Very little structure of any kind. She could discover what she found would work for her."

Although Lily didn't have much professional experience, Friedman says, "She was very clear in her mind about how she saw herself and what she wanted to do. She was nothing like the other comedians around at that time. Even though you didn't know that she was going to be such a huge success, you knew that she had something special. I think the people in the house, who were mainly theater people, could usually sense her uniqueness, too.

"Now bear in mind that she had only halfway developed her talents by this time. When I saw her on 'Laugh-In' a few years later, she was much more polished. I felt, 'So *that*'s what she developed into.' When I finally saw her again in a concert in the seventies, I was totally amazed at the distance she had traveled."

Friedman also recalls: "Lily was very determined about her career, but she was never overly aggressive in promoting herself, the way so many other actresses are. She was never too pushy, so that you didn't think 'Oh, here *she* comes again,' when you saw her."

At this time Lily was living in the East Village, on 5th Street between Second and Third Avenues. "They used my stoop while filming *A Fine Madness* with Sean Connery—I used to peek out the window and watch."

According to Friedman, Lily was very much concerned about the high crime rate in New York. "We once had a conversation about living in New York, and I remember she was really, really frightened. She had three or four locks on her door. I'm talking true anxiety here. . . . So it was no surprise that she wound up living in California."

Lily's work at the Improv led to her finally getting a manager, Irene M. Pinn. "Irene just went bonkers over Lily," recalls Friedman. "She attached herself to Lily quite readily and managed her career for the next ten years. She would coach Lily and watch over her. There was a very trustful relationship between them."

Lily says Irene Pinn "was the only person who ever approached me as a manager who I thought was tasteful. I was mostly approached by people who were wielding a lot of really crass credit cards and cigars and that kind of thing, and I knew they were the type who'd try to tell me what to do, aside from the fact that I didn't want to spend any time with them."

By 1966 Lily was well on her way to finding her style as a performer. Unlike other comics who stick with one successful persona, she was determined to play as many parts as she could dream up. Lily's characters were what interested her; she had no intention of standing up and telling jokes on topical subjects. She had also firmly decided not to do "harsh, ridiculing comedy." Says Lily, "I'm certainly not bland. I want there to be an edge to my humor. But I don't go for the jugular vein. I didn't want to be one of those 'sick' comics."

Despite the heavy odds facing any actress, she felt that because she was unique, she was destined eventually to get the attention she deserved. "Once I got into this performing thing and decided it would be a great way to earn a living, I realized that there were very few comediennes and even fewer who could create material for themselves. Although I thought of myself as an actress, I saw that every actress I knew had to get into a show—and then the show might close. I felt that if I could package myself correctly, I'd have more opportunities to keep working. I really only wanted to work. Plus, I had some kind of compulsion to do it—to make these characters up. But I also had an intuitive feeling that something was going to happen for me in 1966."

As a struggling young actress, Lily hooked up with some struggling young writers in order to help her build her comic repertory. She would have "pitching sessions" with writers, in which they would pitch ideas back and forth for new characters and sketches. Lily recalls one such session with a New York writer, Jim Rusk, that led to the creation of Ernestine, her most popular character. "I told Jim Rusk I wanted to try a little piece about the phone company. His idea was that I'd do a very tough Bronx phone operator. I've still got tapes of me doing Ernestine that way; it's unbelievable how bad I was."

After trying the character out in a few appearances, it suddenly came to Lily that Ernestine's phoney-sweet threats "are an expression of her own highly repressed sexuality. That made her click, in my mind, and the next night, doing her, she just *happened*. Suddenly, without planning it, I physicalized her. My whole body drew in. My mouth pinched in, the voice came from her nose, and the laugh emerged as a snort, because her face wouldn't allow her to really laugh. Suddenly there she was, hiding behind her switchboard, the ultimate obscene phone-caller!"

Although Lily was making real progress in developing her comic skills and characters, her early gigs in New York usually paid very little—and sometimes nothing at all. So in order to make ends meet she was still forced to take other jobs. During the days she would work as an office temporary or a waitress; in the evenings she would pursue her theatrical career. (With her indefatigable supply of energy, holding down two jobs at once was no problem for her, apparently.) "I worked lots of places in New York," she says. "There was the Bun 'n' Burger, the Cookery on Eighth Street—and I worked the counter at the Governor Clinton Coffee Shop, at the Hotel Governor Clinton, for a long time, breakfast and lunch."

Her favorite daytime job was as a waitress. "I was happy being a waitress . . . I think the whole life is so great. I had the most fun working as a waitress at the Howard Johnson's at Forty-ninth Street and Broadway, the one that's closed down now. Working on Broadway was almost like being in show business." She explains: "All the other women were always trying to make their uniforms sexier, but I wore mine very regulation, almost to the ankles—with duty shoes, hairnet—everything."

On one occasion, to liven things up at the restaurant, she announced over the P.A. system: "Attention, diners. Your Howard Johnson Waitress of the Week, Miss Lily Tomlin, is about to make her appearance on the floor. Let's all give her a big hand!" She says the customers were delighted and gave her double her usual tips, but her boss's reaction was somewhat less than enthusiastic.

Beverly Hammond, who worked with Lily at Howard Johnson's, describes her as "a model employee. Lily was always careful that her station looked neat and orderly. She had lots and lots of energy, believe you me. That Lily—she was like one of those perpetual-motion machines. She was happy-go-lucky, always upbeat; she made you feel good to be around her. She did have a sharp tongue, though, sometimes—and she wasn't afraid to speak her mind if some jerk was giving her a hard time. You get every kind of oddball character in a restaurant like that one on Forty-ninth." (Knowing Lily, the presence of a few "oddball characters" must have made the place even more appealing to her.)

Lily's first important break was in 1966, when she was hired to appear on "The Garry Moore Show." At her audition, Moore was impressed by her abilities, but at a loss as to how he could make use of her in his program. "Would you like to see me tap dance?" Lily asked him, then kicked off her shoes and began dancing in her bare feet—the taps had been taped on her soles. Moore was enchanted, and decided to take a chance on her.

But Lily lasted for only three episodes. The producers of "The Garry Moore Show" refused to allow her to do any of her own characterizations. She argued with the writers and called the material she was given "unintelligent." In the end, it didn't matter much, though, for the program was canceled shortly afterward.

The important thing for Lily was that this national exposure brought her into the public eye for the first time. The Ashley-Famous talent agency agreed to represent her, and helped bring more opportunities her way. Some of these jobs were in commercials, which paid well, though Lily says she found working on them to be "totally corrupting" and tried to avoid them whenever she could afford it financially. Her most successful commercial was for Vick's Vapo-Rub.

Meanwhile, Lily went back to the nightclubs and cabarets, and gradually, during 1967 and 1968, began to get some gigs that paid better than her earlier ones had. Tomlin fans may be surprised to learn that on a few occasions she even did her act at the Playboy Club in New York. She also was booked into the Gaslight nightclub in the Village.

One opportunity that turned out to be especially important for Lily was when she became part of the revue at a club called Upstairs at the Downstairs, at 37 West 56th Street. Jeanette Chase, who also worked the Upstairs during 1968, recalls that, "It was sort of spooky when you saw Lily perform. When she did one of her women, it was as if the character had literally taken possession of her. I don't know how she did it, and I don't think Lily knew either.

"Another thing I remember about Lily in those

days was that even if we were having a rough evening, she wouldn't let it get her down. She felt, and made other people feel, a sense of pride in what we did. She felt that being an actress wasn't just any old thing to be doing. It wasn't just another job, it was a real privilege."

Below the Belt was the title of the first revue in which Lily appeared at Upstairs at the Downstairs. In the handbill for the show there is a capsule Tomlin bio, evidently written by Lily herself. It is almost entirely a work of fiction, saying she is a graduate of "Miss Picket's School for Genteel Women in Baton Rouge, Louisiana." Lily is also described as a "superb monologuist, with classical ballet and mime training in Paris"!

In 1968, *The New York Times* critic Vincent Canby gave Lily's career a big boost when he wrote a glowingly favorable notice of her performance in *Photo Finish*, another musical comedy revue at the Upstairs. Canby said, "Miss Tomlin dominates the evening. . . . [Her] abilities are particularly evident in two monologues she wrote for herself. . . . Miss Tomlin may well be headed for the big time."

This review was read by Merv Griffin, who booked Lily for a series of guest spots on his talk show. She got a chance on "The Merv Griffin Show" to do some of her own characterizations on national TV, including that of Lupe, the world's oldest beauty expert. For this bit she would screw up her face in a grotesque grimace, which made her look like a wrinkled crone, while she said, "For years, many people have asked me, 'Lupe, how have you maintained your youthful appearance?'" (Tomlin fans should be aware that a clip from one of these Merv Griffin segments was used in the documentary, *Lily Tomlin*, directed by Joan Churchill and Nicholas Broomfield.)

Canby's prediction that Lily was "headed for the big time" proved to be accurate, for in 1969 she was offered contracts to work regularly on two different television series. The first offer was from "The Music Scene," on ABC. This was a short-lived program featuring six co-hosts (one of whom was Tomlin) and a variety of rock groups. The show premiered September 22, 1969, but lasted only four months—despite guest appearances by James Brown, Janis Joplin, Stevie Wonder, and Crosby, Stills and Nash.

"The Music Scene" was one of those ventures that was virtually doomed from the start, according to Tomlin. "The producers and ABC were fighting constantly," she says. "The people who created the show were ahead of their time, they wanted to do something like 'Saturday Night Live.' But ABC wanted another 'Ed Sullivan Show.'" Tomlin remembers taping a sketch for "The Music Scene" that featured Ernestine: "The ABC censors took it off; they didn't want to offend the phone company. Big corporations look after one another."

Another problem with the show was its unusual format: "The Music Scene" was forty-five minutes long. It was telecast on Monday nights from 7:30 to 8:15, opposite "Gunsmoke." Tomlin lasted through

only the first four episodes; by November the only sur-
viving cast member from the pilot show was David
Steinberg, who became the host for what was left of
the series.

The second TV offer of 1969, on the other hand,
was to change Lily's life dramatically.

CHAPTER 4

"ONE RINGY-DINGY..."

When George Schlatter, the executive producer of "Rowan and Martin's Laugh-In," first caught Tomlin's nightclub act in the summer of 1969, his was the number-one-rated show on television. He had a keen eye for spotting talent, and was immediately impressed by what he saw. He also made a point of viewing kinescopes of her appearances on "The Merv Griffin Show" and "The Garry Moore Show."

But when Schlatter first offered Lily a contract, she was forced to refuse—she had already signed with "The Music Scene." Moreover, she admits that "At first when I had an offer from 'Laugh-In' I was a little nervous, I really didn't want to go. I was scared because I hadn't been that successful on TV, and I was afraid of the other kids, the established cast of 'Laugh-In.' I didn't know them. I thought, 'Oh, they've been there so long'—it was like gong to a new school."

With the almost instantaneous failure of "The Music Scene," however, Lily decided that Schlatter's offer was one she couldn't refuse. She was already in California at that time, so she was able to set up a meeting very soon with Schlatter at his Burbank office. "When I saw George Schlatter . . . that was it. Everything was fine. He understood me and my characters. He was so enthusiastic, he just responded in a second."

Schlatter remembers: "Her talent was so obvious, it was surprising to me that she hadn't yet become a major star. In fact, I felt really lucky to have been the one in the right place at the right time to give her more exposure than she had had before. If 'Laugh-In' hadn't come along for her, I'm sure it was inevitable that she would have found some other vehicle for her talents." Schlatter says that when Tomlin started rehearsing Ernestine, "Everybody onstage, every member of the crew knew that something important was happening. Lily did more for us than we did for her. We needed her desperately."

Before "Laugh-In," Tomlin had never worn a special hairdo or outfit for Ernestine. But the makeup and costume people for the show quickly perceived that the character would be even funnier if she were dressed up in the right way. Tomlin recalls: "I said to the hairdresser, 'I want a hairdo like Loretta Young used to wear,' because I had fancied . . . in my imagination that when I portrayed Ernestine, I really resembled Loretta Young. They made me that wig, which I could not *believe*, it was so perfect!" Someone in the wardrobe department, says Tomlin, then suggested she wear "those forties' blouses, and I already had my own ankle-strap platform shoes."

Tomlin recalls that in October and November of 1969, "I shot about six or seven 'Laugh-In' shows. George Schlatter couldn't decide if he was going to drop me into that last show of '69 or the first show of '70. Then he finally decided to drop me in on December 29, 1969. [Lily has no trouble remembering the date, because she had been told years before by an astrologer that she would become famous sometime late in 1969.] And I literally was famous overnight because of Ernestine, the telephone operator.

"I went to New York over the Christmas hiatus . . . and I saw Ernestine that night on TV. As broad as she was, she looked so real to me. . . . Tuesday [the following day] I went to the theater and people came up to me. People would walk past me and I realized that they were looking at me trying to figure out who I was. And finally they came up to me and said, 'You're that new girl on "Laugh-In" aren't you?' George told me at that time, 'Try to enjoy this, it'll never be this way again.'"

Tomlin had become an instant celebrity. Soon people across the country were familiar with Ernestine's catch phrases: "One ringy-dingy, two ringy-dingys" and "Have I reached the party to whom I am speaking?" Pinch-faced, power-hungry Ernestine was established from her debut snort as one of the most popular characters on 'Laugh-in,' which was viewed each week by forty million Americans.

Reviewers were quick to praise Tomlin as one of the freshest young comediennes to come along in years. The critic for the *National Observer* wrote that she was "one of the few exciting talents to surface in an otherwise underwhelming television season." And in the *New York Post* Cynthia Lowry described her as the "shooting star" of the 1969–70 TV season.

Typically on "Laugh-In" Ernestine delivers, in her nasal whine of a voice, such lines as: "Here at the telephone company we handle eighty-four billion calls a year from everyone, including presidents and the Pope. So we don't need the business of scum like you, who owe us $18.34 from your last month's bill." Or she might respond to an angry customer with endearments such as: "We don't care—we don't have to. We're the phone company."

Some of her most memorable bits are her phone calls to famous people, including Henry Kissinger, Frank Sinatra, William F. Buckley, J. Edgar Hoover, and President Nixon, whom she usually addresses as "Milhous." She particularly likes to harass the rich and powerful, which certainly helped make her popular with TV audiences.

On one occasion Ernestine speaks to Gore Vidal (who made an appearance on the show for this sequence) about the matter of his unpaid phone bill. Unless he sends his check immediately, Ernestine threatens that, "We will send a large burly service man to your house to rip your phone out of the wall. I'd advise you to lock up your liquor—he's a mean drunk. Now wouldn't you prefer to pay up rather than lose your service and possibly the use of one eye?"

Another time she calls up General Motors and says, "A gracious good afternoon, General, and how is Mrs. Motors?" She lets the president of GM know that the telephone company is repairing his hot line to the

White House. "Is that so you can call him before you make an important decision? . . . So that he can call you? . . . But he knows more about shifting gears than anyone else in the country. He believes that what's good for GM is good for the USA—but that's because he's never owned a Corvair." And when Ernestine gets a chance to speak with J. Edgar Hoover, she advises him that he doesn't need to have his FBI agents "skulking around tapping wires. You can get all the information you want from us."

Ernestine reveals the sexual aspect of power as she winds her legs tighter and tighter around each other, her voice rising as she mercilessly lets a customer have it. For the final touch of humiliation she may say, "When you anger me you anger the phone company, and all the power necessary to tie up your lines for the next fifty years!"

Tomlin explains, "Doing Ernestine is really a very sexual experience. I just squeeze myself very tight from the face down." What's more, "The way I see Ernestine is as a very frustrated woman. Her mother wanted her to be a ballet dancer, but she ruined her career by dropping a six-pack of beer on her foot. . . . Ernestine is always tugging at her bra strap. She's a lonely person. And lonely people touch themselves a lot."

Ernestine had become so famous in 1970 that Tomlin was offered $500,000 to do a commercial for AT&T. But she turned it down flat, saying she was "insulted" by the idea. "How could they think I would agree to compromise her in that way?" she told one reporter.

That same year Tomlin received a "Cracked Belle" award from employees of AT&T in Los Angeles. They made her an honorary member of their union, and offered her innumerable suggestions for what she might do in future routines on "Laugh-In."

Lily says there are times when she has to remind herself that Ernestine is actually a fictitious character. "Sometimes I think that Ernestine is a famous real person, like Bette Davis, and I am merely one of the many people who do imitations of her. Sometimes I wonder if she resents me ripping her off, making money from repeating the things she says."

Ernestine is without a doubt Tomlin's best-known characterization. "Ernestine is recognized around the world," explains Lily. "Wherever I go people who recognize me will pucker up their lips and say, 'A gracious hello, Miss Tomlin.'"

Yet Lily has never grown tired of the character. She has usually managed to work her into most of the projects she's been involved with since her "Laugh-In" days. Her TV specials, records, and concerts have almost always included at least a brief cameo appearance by Ernestine. Recently, however, Lily admitted that Ernestine "is heartbroken now, because of the AT&T divestiture. She's lost her power. She's having a mid-life crisis, and it's pretty severe."

At the time of Tomlin's first performance as Ernestine in late 1969, "Laugh-In" was at the height of its popularity. Many of Tomlin's current fans may be unaware of the extraordinary impact the show had in its first few seasons. The format was very different from that of any previous comedy/variety series on

TV. "Laugh-In" was a fast-paced program of virtually nonstop gags—quick flashes of verbal and visual comedy. It featured wacky non sequiturs, topical satire, and cameo appearances by well-known politicians and other celebrities. (During the 1968 campaign, even Richard Nixon came on "Laugh-In" for a brief "Sock it to me!")

Though mild by the standards of the eighties, much of the humor was considered to be more than a little risqué at the time. In fact, "Rowan and Martin's Laugh-In" (along with "The Smothers Brothers Comedy Hour") was instrumental in breaking many of the taboos that the television networks had rigidly enforced during the fifties and sixties. For example, in the premiere episode of "Laugh-In," on January 22, 1968, one joke was "The bombing of the Central Highlands in Vietnam will stop—when the Viet Cong reach the outskirts of Paris." This was a highly controversial bit of material at the time, since it pretty bluntly implied that the conduct of American policy in Vietnam was inept, to say the least.

George Schlatter was the man chiefly responsible for making "Laugh-In" such an influential program. He put together the team of writers and performers, nearly all of whom were little-known to the public, and established an atmosphere in which they felt free to experiment and make all kinds of outlandish suggestions. Schlatter would let the writers and performers go ahead and try just about anything they could think up (anything, that is, which the censors wouldn't object to).

"Each of us brought our own thing to the show,"

explains Henry Gibson, one of the stars of "Laugh-In" in the early seasons. "We had developed most of the characters we did before we were hired. . . . So George Schlatter wasn't so much the creator of the show all by himself as he was the catalyst that got things going."

Another popular member of the cast, Jo Anne Worley, says, "We were encouraged to bring in our own creative material and keep the spots going. There was no jealousy. If I thought one of my lines sounded more like another character's, I'd say so and she'd do it."

Schlatter explains that part of his intention was to create a comedy show that was designed especially for television. Most TV comedy or variety programs, then as now, could just as easily be performed in a theater. Most sitcoms, as a matter of fact, are still performed before a studio audience. The cameras are used to record what happens onstage: the process is essentially one of filming a play. "Laugh-In" on the other hand, would be impossible anyplace but on TV. Each hour-long show consisted of three or four hundred separate shots—many of them only a fraction of a second long. Most of the "scenes" lasted for about ten or twenty seconds.

"It was a milestone," says Schlatter, "the first new creation in TV, because it was not a radio show done so you could see it, not a nightclub act or theater show or motion picture. It was a pure television form using the techniques available to television and taking into account the whole accelerated learning process, the whole element of future shock on our society."

Seen today, "Laugh-In" retains much of the fresh-ness that it had twenty years ago. The quick-paced for-mat of the show is just as much of a departure from most TV series in the eighties as it was in the sixties. Some of the writing displays genuine wit. Probably the best element of the show, however, is the acting. The comic performances of Goldie Hawn, Arte Johnson, Henry Gibson, and, of course, Lily Tomlin are very often delightful, even when the material is less than sparkling.

But even the most avid fan of "Laugh-In" would have to admit that the show is wildly uneven. An imaginative sketch is often followed by one which is so corny that viewers can't help but groan while watching it.

Many of the jokes on the show are visual rather than verbal. A bikini-clad girl dances the boogaloo: when the camera zooms in on her we see that she is painted from head to toe with silly graffiti. In another running gag, British comedienne Judy Carne tries ev-erything she can think of to avoid being doused with water while a chorus of voices in the background shouts, "Sock it to me!"

Some of the one-liners appear written in letters superimposed on the screen, much like subtitles. For instance, during a scene about a completely unrelated topic, viewers may see these bits of graffiti appearing out of nowhere: "George Wallace—Your Sheets Are Ready" or "This Is Your Slum—Keep It Clean" or "Forest Fires Prevent Bears."

Many of the scenes are short takes in which an actor or actress will recite a quick punch line, such as,

"If Shirley Temple Black had married Tyrone Power, she'd be Shirley Black Power." The announcer for "Laugh-In," Gary Owens, also gets into the act fairly often. At the beginning of one episode we see him saying, on-camera, "The preceding program which follows was immediately prerecorded to give the cast time to disguise themselves before leaving the studio."

One of the most popular members of the cast is Arte Johnson, who dresses up as a Nazi and says "verrry interesting" a lot. He also appears as a dirty old man and as a guru who is fond of giving off-the-wall advice. "Man who speaketh with forked tongue should never kiss a balloon," he says in one episode.

And then there's Goldie Hawn, usually playing a dizzy blond cream puff who is always blowing her lines. Typically, she will giggle, bite her lip, and say something like this: "I don't like Viet Cong, because in the movie he nearly wrecked the Empire State Building."

Presiding as the masters of ceremonies for all of these strange goings-on are Dan Rowan and Dick Martin. Prior to "Laugh-In," they had worked together as nightclub comics in Las Vegas. Much of their humor is reminiscent of the comedy team of Dean Martin and Jerry Lewis; Rowan plays the straight man, while Dick Martin is the "dumb" one who cracks most of the jokes.

Lily Tomlin's popularity continued to rise throughout the 1970–71 television season as she kept making her weekly appearances on "Laugh-In." She gradually introduced more members of her gallery of characters, broadening her repertoire with portrayals of Edith Ann, the Tasteful Lady, Suzy Sorority, and many others.

Next to Ernestine, Edith Ann was Lily's most popular character in the early seventies. Edith Ann is an extremely uninhibited five-year-old girl, with stringy hair and chocolate smears on her face, who often sits in an oversized rocking chair. She has trouble pronouncing the "th" sound, and loves to tell embarrassing truths about her family to total strangers. She spends much of her time trying to find a spot where she can play doctor with her six-year-old boyfriend, Junior Phillips. Edith Ann's favorite phrase is "and that's the truth." Lily clearly has a great time portraying Edith Ann; she uses a raspy voice and likes to stick out her tongue at the audience whenever she gets the chance. Lily describes her, quite accurately, as "a wonderful little monster."

Lily remembers she "probably had thought about Edith Ann for years without being conscious of it. I just wanted to do a child. Then I met a little girl in Pennsylvania. Her name was Charlene and she was a darling. Her father worked for the hotel where I was staying. He invited me to his home for dinner and there she was. She had this speech mannerism where anything that ended with a 'th' would cause her to make this little, delicate ruffling sound. She recognized me from television and she talked, talked, talked. She had this big stuffed snake and every now and then she'd say, 'Snake takes a bath.' I wanted that speaking mannerism of hers, so I tried to think of a phrase that ended in 'th'; that's how I came up with 'and that's the truth.'"

Tomlin's own favorite Edith Ann routine is the one in which she talks about her ideas of what it would be like to go to heaven. "A kid can do whatever she wants to in heaven," says Edith Ann. "She can put on lipstick and she can talk to the animals because animals talk in heaven. And in heaven your mother has to go to bed real early—and that's the truth."

Some of the writers and producers for "Laugh-In" didn't appreciate Edith Ann at first. Lily had to do a considerable amount of arguing with them in order to get Edith Ann on the show regularly. "I had some trouble making her scruffy," explains Tomlin. "The 'Laugh-In' producers wanted her to look like Shirley Temple. . . . They'd ask questions like, 'Is she retarded?' 'Why is her hair so stringy?' 'Is her face dirty?' 'Why does she talk so funny—is that a raspberry?' But I knew she was a real person . . . and I wanted very much to be able to do her."

Mrs. Earbore, the Tasteful Lady, is one of Tomlin's best characterizations from "Laugh-In." She's a takeoff on the snooty country club women of Grosse Pointe, one of the wealthiest suburbs of Detroit, Michigan. In a typical sequence, Mrs. Earbore says, "Our club has always had a tasteful policy of extending invitation memberships to minority groups. We did have to cancel it last week, however, when much to our surprise, one of them accepted."

Another amusing Tomlin portrayal from "Laugh-In" is the Fast Talker. She's a sweet young woman who speaks at such a breathless pace, and with such gushing enthusiasm, that it's impossible to make sense of most of what she is trying to say.

Lily was "never too crazy" about her character Suzy Sorority of the Silent Majority. "I only did her on 'Laugh-In' because I traded her off for Edith Ann. . . . When I met with the writers at the beginning of one of the seasons, I brought in three or four new characters, and I had in my mind—I knew—who I wanted to do, but just to keep the momentum going, I threw in a couple of secondary characters and, unfortunately, they glommed on to one of those—Suzie. Who was never a character, really, only a concept." Suzie Sorority has "a good look about her and she's identifiable. But she's a nonperson. She parrots what she hears. She's completely adopted her parents' values. If she's not an anachronism, then she's a throwback. She wishes it were 1955 and everything were beautiful."

Suzy Sorority has long blond hair and huge eyeglasses and speaks in a timid, thin-as-an-eggshell voice. She describes herself as "a charter member of the Y.A.C.F., that's Young Americans for Connie Francis. Now there's a person who has a lot of problems—like what to wear to entertain the troops, things like that. But you don't see Connie shooting glue or smoking acid or getting low or smelling those L.S.M.F.T. tablets. No sir, when something upsets Connie, she just sings her little heart out and the troubles of the world . . . disappear."

As Tomlin continued to bring in new characters, viewers of "Laugh-In" became increasingly familiar with her brand of comedy. What she liked to do, it soon became apparent, was to portray "people who don't fit in and think they do. That's what's so beautiful about them. None of the characters I do think there's anything wrong with them, and there isn't—to me, at least."

Lily's favorite characters are those, like Edith Ann, who think very well of themselves. As Lily explains, "I always want them to be strong. I never like to do anybody who's defeated. . . . The person I love most of all is somebody who conventionally looks out of place, and who thinks she's wonderful. There's nobody more beautiful than that, somebody who's just a real character. They give you a lift. It's like when I meet people who disarm me with their truthfulness. It's such a gift from them to express something that all of us are afraid to express, to get it out in the air. It's such a present, you get high from it." The essential Lily Tomlin character, then, is a woman who recognizes no authority outside of herself, who fearlessly and unrepentently does whatever she feels like doing.

Asked to say what it was that made Tomlin's characterizations on "Laugh-In" so memorable, George Schlatter replies: "There is bite in her comedy. But she never goes for a joke outside of the character. She won't burn herself out because people are interested in her characters, who are real people to her. . . . Lily knows their histories, families, habits, and fantasies."

With her television success, Tomlin moved to Southern California, where she has lived ever since. In 1970 and 1971 she lived in what she calls a "chaotic" beach house in Malibu. Although she received some hefty pay raises during her later seasons on "Laugh-In," Tomlin says she didn't make all that much in her first year on the show. She is sorry that she didn't become famous a little sooner, for "one lifetime regret I have is that . . . I never got to buy my daddy a Cadillac. He died [in 1970] before I could afford it. He was a wonderful character. He died from alcoholism, but I loved him. He'd always say, 'Lily, some day you're going to buy your old daddy a Cadillac' . . . I always thought there would be time for that."

Remembering her father and her rapid rise to fame on "Laugh-In," Lily tells this story: "My parents had moved to Fort Wayne, Indiana, because my father's factory had been relocated. And we went out to this restaurant/bar. I had been on the show for about a month at this time. A few people were looking at me, but they couldn't put it together. So when the waitress came over to us, my father asked if she knew who I was. The woman said she guessed I was his daughter. 'Damn right,' he said, then insisted I get up and sing a song. I was too embarrassed and kept refusing. But I will never forget how he responded to my embarrassment. He said, 'Babe, you got to learn how to be popular.' And that has been a difficult lesson for me. When you are primarily a people watcher, it is sometimes very uncomfortable to realize you are the one being watched."

CHAPTER 5

THIS IS
A RECORDING

In 1971 Tomlin took another important step forward in her career when she made her first comedy album, entitled—appropriately enough—*This Is a Recording*, which was released on the Polydor label. For that LP, she performed some of her funniest Ernestine routines (written by Lily, along with a number of "Laugh-In" writers). And not only did *This Is a Recording* become a gold record, it was a smashing success with the critics. The LP won the Grammy Award for Best Comedy Record, and it was also named the year's best comedy record by both *Cashbox* and *Record World* magazines.

Even Tomlin says she was surprised at how well *This Is a Recording* was received. "I never expected to do a record. I thought I was too visual."

The LP was recorded live at The Ice House, a small Pasadena coffeehouse where Tomlin performed often in the early seventies. She used The Ice House as a place to try out material for her TV and concert appearances. In 1971 she told a reporter for *Cue*, "I like to play small places like coffeehouses. . . . You can act foolish. Young people are so much looser." Lily explained that she didn't have "an act as such. . . . What I have is a body of material that I draw from. I hope, too, that I'll think of something unique for that night or audience."

This Is a Recording features some very entertaining monologues, including one of Ernestine's run-ins with J. Edgar Hoover. "Mr. Hoover, this is Miss Tomlin from the telephone company, and it is my duty to discuss with you some of the abuses of your instrument . . . Yes, it does sound rather un-American, doesn't it? . . . Now then, Mr. Hoover, I have your file here before me . . . Oh yes, I'm sure you have a file on me, too. After all, turnabout is fair play . . . Yes, it does sound a little perverted, doesn't it? . . . Mr. Hoover, I have a delicate problem. I find that you and your agents have indulged in the illegal and unfair practice of—wire-tapping . . . How do I know? From listening in on your calls, that's how I know."

Another highlight of the album is when Lily briefly steps out of the character of Ernestine and, speaking for herself, gives listeners some interesting advice on paying their phone bills: "Yes, there is a way to strike back. When you get your telephone bill, you know that it's on an IBM card. So take your IBM card and . . . put it in a basin of tepid water about an inch deep. Add a teaspoon of Snowy Bleach. Then soak your card for six to eight minutes—not so it gets pulpy, just so it's saturated. Then take a steam iron and iron your card dry. You'll find that the holes will shrink, just a little teeny bit . . ."

As the 1971–72 and 1972–73 TV seasons wore on, Tomlin became increasingly dissatisfied with the jokes she was performing on "Laugh-In." Her characters "were losing their integrity [due] to bad scripts and overexposure." She felt that what was happening to Ernestine was symptomatic of the problems in general with the show. The writers were supplying her with "material that was just too low for Ernestine—garbage, really. She worked fine as long as she was pegged to the phone company's power, as long as she called truly powerful people, went after big targets, Nixon, J. Edgar Hoover, whom only she has access to. When you start having her call Joe Namath about his knee, you're losing her point, the intelligence and integrity of her concept just goes. I was constantly protecting her by then. I'd keep saying, 'I can't do her, week after week, when the material's not good enough.'"

There's no question that the quality of "Laugh-In" slipped in the later seasons. The program suffered largely because most of the original cast members had departed, including Goldie Hawn, Judy Carne, Arte Johnson, and Henry Gibson. Another problem was that George Schlatter left the show in 1971, and was replaced by Paul Keyes.

Tomlin made no secret of the fact that she disapproved of the way Keyes was running the show. (Meanwhile, he was quoted in the press as saying she was "someone who does not take criticism well.") Tomlin successfully sued the producers of "Laugh-In" in 1972, establishing that she was the "sole owner" of all the characters she had created. She started to look for ways of getting out of her contract. During the same period, she was receiving offers from CBS and ABC ("Laugh-In" was on NBC) to host her own specials. So when the series finally went off the air on May 14, 1973, she was not at all unhappy over the turn of events.

While Tomlin was still starring on "Laugh-In," she met Jane Wagner, who was to become her most important collaborator, as well as her best friend, in the years to follow. She was impressed by *J.T.*, Wagner's Peabody award-winning script for a TV movie about a black boy growing up in Harlem, and Lily suggested they might work together. About *J.T.*, Lily says, "It was naturalistic and yet it had a kind of heightened realism that was poetic and lyrical and terribly inventive."

Wagner and Tomlin soon discovered that they shared a Southern, working-class background: Tomlin's family was from Kentucky and Wagner grew up in Tennessee. As a child, Wagner says she was painfully shy. Her home town was Morristown, Tennessee, which is near the Great Smoky Mountains. "I come right out of Southern-novelist country—you know, Carson McCullers and James Agee and the rest," says Wagner. When she was young, she felt that Tennessee Williams had destroyed her ambition of becoming a writer, "because I thought, 'What's he left for anyone else to do?'" So she made up her mind to try instead to be an actress.

When Wagner, age eighteen, first came to New York, she knew no one in the city and had had very little experience as a performer. She took a room at the YWCA, where she lived for three years. For the next ten years, she experienced a series of setbacks and near-misses in Manhattan. Her acting career never really took off; she eventually turned to songwriting. A song about a boy named J.T. was rejected by record producers who said it was too long, so she reworked the story into a television play. She then sent it to an agent who sold it to CBS.

Before collaborating with Tomlin, Wagner had never written comedy. She remembers thinking, "Working with Lily would be a stretch for me. We got together for the first time in Pasadena during the Rose Parade. . . . Lily wanted me to help her enrich the character of Edith Ann."

It didn't take long for them to realize that they worked together very well. "In the deepest ways we connect, we want the same things," explains Wagner. "We just disagree sometimes on how to get there."

Lily talks about Jane in glowing terms: "We share similar feelings about people and about the world. She's able to verbalize it and I'm able to physicalize it. She writes satirically but tenderly, and she loves farce and black comedy and broad slapstick. When you put all this together and make an audience laugh and be moved, it's just glorious."

To date, Wagner and Tomlin have collaborated on the writing of four Emmy Award–winning TV specials, three Grammy-nominated comedy LPs, and the play *Appearing Nitely*. Wagner also wrote the scripts for the movies *Moment by Moment* (which she directed) and *The Incredible Shrinking Woman*. Furthermore, Wagner was the sole author of *The Search* for *Signs of Intelligent Life in the Universe*, Tomlin's most recent Broadway hit. As time has passed, Lily has more and more left the writing to Jane—so that their collaboration in the eighties has usually been one in which Jane writes the words and Lily performs them. On the whole, Wagner's writing is more even and more polished than Tomlin's, whose greatest talents are for inventing characters and for bringing them to life as an actress.

"Jane is a true writer," explains Lily. "If you say to her, 'Write about this salt shaker,' she'll find a way to write about it." Lily says she often feels in awe of Jane's talents. "I'm continually amazed that Jane can sit down and write something, and go so far beyond anything I could imagine."

Lily has never actually stated clearly in public whether or not she is a bisexual or a lesbian, but she has talked about the issue on several occasions. While it's not always easy to tell when she's being flippant, when she's making a political statement, or when she's being serious, most of her comments seem sincere. In some of her concerts from the early seventies, for example, she would say, "In the fifties . . . no one was gay then, we were shy."

She also raised quite a few eyebrows as a result of one of her comments in a 1973 interview with *The New York Times*. Lily was criticizing the remarks that actress Maria Schneider (most famous for her role in *Last Tango in Paris*) had previously made in another interview with the *Times*. Schneider had confessed to having gone to bed with fifty men and twenty women. In Lily's interview with the *Times*, she said that, in her own case, those figures that Schneider mentioned should be reversed. "Instead of fifty men and twenty women," said Lily, "write that I've had fifty women and twenty men. If I'm going to go out on a bisexual limb, I don't want to play safe by listing more men than women. That was *disgusting* of Maria."

Jack Kroll of *Newsweek* later asked Lily to expand on her comment to the *Times*. She told Kroll, "I thought that piece was so sleazy. It's like it was okay to say you're bisexual in *The New York Times* as long as there were more men than women. The truth is that you should love anyone, man or woman. But because of the culture, you can't even be affectionate with friends, women or men. I think you choose your friends, and their sexuality has to have a part in it. Their sexuality is something so central to them—you want to embrace it. I have friends, men and women, that I feel very close to. But, as advanced as some of them are, I am careful about how I relate to them. Sometimes I forget myself and get all nuzzly and throw myself totally into their bodies. I forget that it's not exactly okay, that everyone's a little scared or a little unsure. I wish everything weren't such a big deal. You can't be tender, and tender is really it, tender is great."

As far as the question of getting married or having children is concerned, Lily recalls: "One time I was on 'The Tonight Show' and Johnny Carson asked me if I wanted children. I was still on 'Laugh-In,' so I knew my answer had import with the TV audience. 'No,' I said, telling the truth as my heart pounded, 'having a child is not a major objective in my life.'" And in a

1970 interview with *The New York Times,* she said, "I don't think much about getting married. I've passed that point."

Tomlin and Wagner's first project together was an LP released in 1972 by Polydor records, *And That's the Truth.* It features two characters—precocious Edith Ann and a woman the little girl calls "Lady." Both parts are, of course, played by Tomlin.

A typical moment from the record is when Edith Ann remarks, "I didn't ask to be born . . . if I did, Mama would have said no." Edith Ann also makes this interesting comment on what happens when people get angry: "First, your face gets just like a fist, and then your heart gets like a bunch of bees and flies up and stings your brain . . . And then your eyes are like dark clouds looking for trouble. And your blood is like a tornado and then you have bad weather inside your body."

According to Edith Ann, God has a television set on which He monitors the activities of every person on earth. When she's afraid that He is viewing her, she does "a little commercial" for herself. Edith Ann worries that vegetables may become angry when we eat them. She puts mouthwash into her dog's water dish, because she wants him to smell good when she kisses him.

Reviewers had some very complimentary things to say about *And That's the Truth.* The critic for *Stereo Review* wrote, "Edith Ann, in her phonographic debut, is a far more interesting child than she has been in her cameo TV appearances. . . . [I am] lost in admiration at the inventiveness of the script and

Miss Tomlin's unfailing skill at sustaining an exacting routine, bringing it off without one false note to mar the illusion. And that's the truth."

Writing for *The New York Times*, Ellen Cohn pointed out, "With her Edith Ann record Tomlin moved away from arbitrarily strung-together routines, the standard format for comedy recording. . . . Edith Ann, no longer merely a smart-alecky kid, becomes a vehicle for revealing the loneliness of childhood, the naked need for approval and admiration."

On March 16, 1973, *The Lily Tomlin Show*, a sixty-minute comedy special, was broadcast by CBS. It was Tomlin's first special, and it remains one of her best. (To date she has starred in seven specials.) The show featured Tomlin along with some other noted performers, such as Richard Pryor and Richard Crenna. *The Lily Tomlin Show* earned a highly respectable Nielsen rating of 23.5 and was later nominated for an Emmy.

Yet the program nearly wasn't broadcast. Several sketches were eliminated by CBS censors, such as a routine entitled "War Games," featuring Mrs. Beasley, which Tomlin says was "a nice woman's statement—anti-war and anti–war-toys." The skit dealt with the violent toys that are sold to children. At one point Mrs. Beasley told her son—and this was the most controversial line—"Come on, leg or no leg, supper's on the table."

Tomlin explains, "CBS thought it was offensive. The networks feel certain things don't belong in variety shows, but what I've always hated about variety shows is that they have no variety."

Also controversial was her decision to hire Richard Pryor, who had the reputation of being a comedian unafraid of tackling subjects considered "objectionable" by the networks. Lorne Michaels, a writer on three of Tomlin's specials and later the producer of "Saturday Night Live," says, "By 1973 it was pretty much acknowledged that Richard Pryor was the funniest man on the planet—but also the most dangerous. Lily put her career in jeopardy over corporate objections and got him to perform and write."

In one of the most amusing sketches, Pryor plays a wino named Lightnin' Bug Johnson who gets stuck in an elevator with Tomlin's Tasteful Lady. She's appalled by his disheveled appearance, his coarse sense of humor, and the smell of his cheap booze, but she does her best to keep up her composure. After they get out, she says, "Keep in touch, Mr. Lightning Bug."

At the beginning of the program Lily comes out and delivers a short monologue in which she explains, among other things, how she arrived at the title for the special. It was called The Lily Tomlin Show, she says, because, "If someone gave you a show, who would you name it for?"

A new Tomlin character, Bobbi-Jeanine, an organist in a cocktail lounge, is featured in another bit. Bobbi-Jeanine talks in a stream of show-biz clichés and song lyrics, punctuating her words with chords on her keyboard. She says, "Hello, I'm Bobbi-Jeanine [music: "A Pretty Girl Is Like a Memory"]. I'm here to entertain you [chord], you [chord], and especially . . . you [series of notes], because, ladies and gentlemen, what the world needs now is love [chord] sweet love [series of notes]."

John J. O'Connor, reviewing the special for *The New York Times*, wrote, "Tomlin . . . is a delightful comedy actress, shifting easily between monologues about herself and a number of characterizations, several familiar from 'Laugh-In.'"

Yet in spite of good ratings and reviews, CBS executives were hesitant about letting her do another special. When they finally gave her the okay, it was with the warning that she should be more conventional the second time around. Executives were afraid that she would fail to appeal to Middle America.

But Tomlin was not intimidated and paid little or no attention to their suggestions. She taped "War Games" again, and CBS dropped it again. Another sketch, entitled "Juke and Opal," featuring Tomlin and Pryor, also ran into strong opposition from the network. Tomlin portrayed Opal, the proprietor of a café, and Pryor was her friend Juke, a guy strung out on methadone. ("Juke and Opal" was written by Jane Wagner.) CBS finally decided to leave it in the show, but they "sweetened" the routine with canned laughter and pushed it back to the end of the hour, while moving less controversial material to the beginning. The thinking was that if viewers were offended that late in the show, it wouldn't matter since they had already seen most of the commercials.

Lily, this second special, was telecast in November of 1973. Besides getting favorable ratings and rave reviews, *Lily* was the first of Tomlin's specials to receive an Emmy Award. In fact, *Lily* wound up earning two Emmies—for "Best writing for a comedy, variety, or music special" and for "Best comedy, variety, or music special." This time, Alan Alda joined Tomlin and Pryor in the cast; the producer was Herb Sargent; and the writers were Lorne Michaels, Tomlin, Wagner, and several others.

Still, CBS executives decided that they had had enough of Tomlin, and didn't offer her another special. Lily says she had to try hard not to be bitter about the experience. "CBS thought both my specials were peculiar, and they were very reluctant to let the second . . . go on at all. At the last minute it was shown to a bigwig, and he only had a vague idea as to what I do, and he was horrified. I felt sorry for the underlings, because they had to turn on me and in his presence call me up and pretend that they had no knowledge of what I had been doing. . . . [The executives] are all so cynical about the American public. 'Remember Dubuque,' they like to say, implying that 'the simpletons out there won't understand anything but one-liners.'"

Following her difficult experience with CBS, Tomlin tried her luck at ABC. Her first effort for the new network was *Lily,* which was broadcast February 21, 1975. Her co-star was Richard Dreyfuss, and the writing was done mostly by the same team that had worked with her on the two specials for CBS.

A highpoint of the ABC special is a sketch in which Tomlin plays a woman who is perplexed by the behavior of a man who proposes marriage to her after their first date. He even goes and gets his parents to meet her, and his mother confides to the Tomlin character, "Most of the time we don't even meet the girls he makes it with."

"Miss Tomlin, warm and friendly, is almost embarrassingly perceptive about foibles, her own and everybody else's," said John J. O'Connor, in the *Times*. "It might be disturbing if she weren't so funny."

Lily's next Emmy Award–winner (for "Best writing for a comedy, variety, or music special") was *Lily Tomlin*, first shown on ABC July 25, 1975. *Variety's* reviewer commented that this special "was high-quality, sophisticated fare, and evidently too restrained and tasteful to appeal to network program execs, who want variety shows to aim at a lower denominator." Both *Lily* and *Lily Tomlin* had been originally intended as pilots for a new ABC variety series, but network executives never gave the go-ahead for Tomlin to produce more episodes.

Mrs. Beasley, the "perfect housewife" from Calumet City, Illinois, is one of the most noteworthy portrayals in *Lily Tomlin*. In a routine featuring her, viewers are treated to a send-up of women's hairspray commercials. Mrs. Beasley shows us how Sta-Put keeps her hair in place, no matter what the situation. She proves this by sitting in a chair that is pushed through a car wash. Her body is soaked, but her hair appears to have made it through unscathed.

From her specials, we can easily see that Tomlin's style of comedy is well-suited to the medium of television. It's a good context in which to present her gallery of characters. In close-ups, the camera catches those subtleties of expression and gesture that may be missed in a large theater. What's more, in one TV special she can play a dozen different roles, while in a movie she would usually be limited to one. Some of Tomlin's best work has been in her TV specials—especially *The Lily Tomlin Show* in 1973 and *Lily: Sold Out* in 1981. It's a pity that these programs have been shown so rarely since they were first broadcast.

"We'd work seventeen, eighteen hours a day on those specials," remembers Lorne Michaels. "But the twentieth take would always be a miracle. She's an anomaly compared to most comic actors, who read off cue cards and go for the instant laugh."

Besides her many appearances on TV in the early to mid-seventies, Tomlin also went on several concert tours around the country, giving performances at such varied places as the Atlanta Music Hall, the Shoreham Hotel in Washington, and Carnegie Hall and the Bitter End nightclub in New York. Probably the most acclaimed of all her live performances, though, was at the Royal Variety Show in London, where she entertained members of the British royal family with her portrayal of Ernestine.

Lily is well known not only for her strong convictions about her work but for her strong social and political convictions. She's a staunch feminist who refuses to do any sketches that demean women, and she has consistently demonstrated her support for various liberal causes. Tomlin was outspoken in her opposition to the Vietnam War, and she has been involved in several campaigns for Democratic Party candidates, such as George McGovern.

Yet she has rarely attempted to lampoon political figures; instead, she prefers to stick with her own characters. "I couldn't really do the Nixons," she explained in a 1970 interview, "because I'd have to stop and think what made them that way. I can't work or think angry."

Lily considers very carefully the possible effects that her work will have on the people who see it. As an example of the type of response she seeks to avoid, she vividly remembers what happened early in her career when she was doing a nightclub routine about a John Bircher. After the performance, a "Neanderthal boyfriend" of one of the other women in the show came up to her and said: "That was great. I hate those goddamn niggers as much as you do." Says Lily, "It really shocked me, and I've never done that character again."

Though clearly a liberal, Lily feels she doesn't have a "radical sensibility." Moreover, she is uncomfortable around those who are "fanatically devoted to a cause to the point where they have blinders on and feel that the end justifies the means." She adds, "I don't want to be a spokesperson for any one group. If I'm playing for a special interest audience—feminists, activists, whatever—and I feel them getting too chummy with me, I'll just go on a reverse kick. I start satirizing myself."

The cause that Lily is the most passionate about, however, clearly is feminism. When asked what impact the women's movement has had on her career, she responds, "If it hadn't been for the women's movement, people would call it my hobby."

Lily was a guest on "The Dick Cavett Show" on the occasion in 1972 when Chad Everett referred to his wife as his "property." Lily immediately got up and walked out of the studio. "There are times when I lose my temper, when I'm volatile—but this wasn't one of those," she explains. "I was very calm as I left. . . . It was a perfectly pure act. I felt angels walked me off."

Another notable incident occurred when she was being interviewed by Barbara Walters on the "Today" show. Lily was describing the hairspray commercial that Mrs. Beasley performs in the 1975 *Lily Tomlin* special when Walters remarked, quite casually, "I do a hairspray commercial, too." Lily was plainly dismayed. "You do? What about the environment?" After an uneasy silence, Walters changed the subject.

Lily's next comedy album, *Modern Scream*, was based on material that she had been developing for several years in her concerts. *Modern Scream* is consistently entertaining, with ten different Tomlin impersonations in evidence.

"Lucille, the Rubber Freak," one of the most inspired bits on any of her albums, is the confession of a middle-aged housewife who starts out chewing rubber bands and gradually finds herself becoming an addict. She knew she had reached the depths of degradation when "the garden hose went." But in the end she rehabilitates herself, proudly declaring, "I'm no longer a woman obsessed with an unnatural craving. I'm just another normal, healthy, very socially acceptable alcoholic."

In "Sister Boogie Woman," Lily transforms herself into a Southern evangelist whose every word seems filled with a passionate fervor for the Lord. She yells herself hoarse as she preaches one of her sermons. "Boogie's not a meanin', boogie's a feelin'! Boogie takes the question marks out of your eyes, puts little exclamation marks in their place! Are you on my beam? . . . Boogie's when the rest of the world is lookin' you straight in the eye, sayin' you'll never be able to make it, and you got your teeth in a jar and those teeth say, 'Yes I can, yes I can, yes I can!' I say think of yourself as a potato chip and life as a dip! I say think of yourself as a chicken leg and life as Shake 'n' Bake!" (It seems a safe bet that the Tasteful Lady is not a member of Sister Boogie Woman's congregation.)

Mrs. Beasley also shows up on the album, with some words of wisdom. "I'm not here to sell you a product, but to give you some good consumer advice," she says. "Some of us when confronted with a choice of material goods, act a little like junkies. If you are the type of person who goes to the market for a quart of milk and a loaf of bread, and comes back with a Teflon teakettle, a popcorn popper, a gym suit, toothpicks, potholders, a mop, and some bean dip . . . chances are you are an impulse buyer. Especially if you got those items and forgot the milk and bread. It's nothing to be ashamed of, but something to be concerned about. I know—I was an impulse shopper of the worst kind. I would buy anything at eye level."

Not every review of *Modern Scream* was favorable, but nearly all the critics had to at least tip their caps to Tomlin's obvious talents. Shaun Considine said in *The New York Times*, "Although she gets bogged down on this album, caught up in her own traffic jam, Tomlin still has her shining moments: she is a mistress of satire."

When "Saturday Night Live" had its debut in 1975, producer Lorne Michaels immediately thought of Tomlin as a possible guest host. She accepted his offer, and came on one of the earliest—and best—episodes of the show. Michaels is very fond of the specials he worked on with Tomlin. "They were a model for what we were trying to do on 'Saturday Night.' They had the word *experimental* written all over them. . . . Instead of the usual crooners and chorus girls, her shows had political stuff and mood pieces and moments of truth."

Marilyn Miller, one of the writers for "Saturday Night Live," says that the women on the staff tried especially hard to make Tomlin's show a good one. Most comedy programs are male-dominated, she explains, but with Tomlin in control the atmosphere was very different.

The best example of how she made a difference is the sketch on the show in which a group of women construction workers ogle a rather scantily clad man. Obviously, the humor comes from the reversal of the tradition situation. "Hey, beefcake," says the Tomlin character. "Sweetheart, strut your stuff in front of Gilda . . . You little tease, you little juicy buns." The man becomes increasingly uncomfortable. Finally, he tells them, "Okay, just hold on a minute. Knock it off. Men have feelings too, you know."

The skit worked very well, but the trouble was that none of the guys on the show wanted to perform in it. John Belushi, whom it was written for, absolutely refused to play the part. Dan Aykroyd was nearly as resistant: he made it plain that the idea of wearing a revealing outfit while being humiliated by a group of women did not at all appeal to him. Eventually, Tomlin and Michaels managed to change his mind, and he looked appropriately ill at ease during his performance of this routine.

Also of special interest is Tomlin's opening monologue, in which she delivers some random thoughts and observations. "I wonder what it would be like if we all became what we had wanted to become when we grew up," she says. "Imagine a world filled with nothing but firemen, cowboys, nurses, and ballerinas." Furthermore, "I wonder why there isn't a special name for the *tops* of your feet." And, "How come when you're the last person in a line that isn't moving, and someone comes along and stands behind you, you feel a lot better?"

The year 1975 turned out to be pivotal for Tomlin. Not only did she win an Emmy, make her third comedy record, and the first of her popular appearances on NBC's "Saturday Night Live," but, even more important, she made her first movie.

MODERN SCREEN

Not many actors or actresses can boast of making a better first impression in the movies than Tomlin did in *Nashville*. Her performance as Linnea, a devoted mother who has an adulterous affair with a rock singer, was nominated for an Academy Award. Tomlin's affecting work in this film provided clear evidence that she was not just a skillful comic caricaturist, but a real actress who could handle a part with sensitivity.

Yet Tomlin says she was hesitant at first about being in *Nashville*. "When I got the part I thought, 'I'm not *her*.' But as I looked at everybody else and saw how perfect they were, I decided Altman [the director] couldn't be wrong about me."

Nashville was one of the most talked-about movies of the seventies: many critics felt that it was the most original American film to come along in years. The main target of the satire in *Nashville* is the country-music world, yet just about every aspect of

American life, from political campaigns to sexual mores, is subjected to a less than flattering examination. There is no easily summarizable plot, only a series of related incidents. Over the course of the film we gradually get to know twenty-four major characters, whose lives crisscross each other's, all heading for the final scene that brings everyone together.

The setting is Nashville, Tennessee, during the 1976 presidential campaign. A third-party candidate, Hal Philip Walker, whom we never actually see, is planning a huge outdoor rally to boost his campaign. (Walker is a fanatical defender of free enterprise and his candidacy seems to have been modeled, in part, after George Wallace's.) Walker's public relations man, John Triplette (played by Michael Murphy), tries to enlist the leading stars of country music to appear at the campaign rally. The most prominent of these are Barbara Jean (Ronee Blakley), the "first lady of country music," and Haven Hamilton (Henry Gibson), the top male singer. Throughout the five days immediately before the big rally, we follow Triplette in his wheelings and dealings: along the way we're introduced to the variety of characters representing different walks of life in Nashville. There are would-be musicians, greedy managers, and a host of unsavory types tangentially involved in the country and western scene.

In 1972 Altman hired Joan Tewkesbury to write the screenplay for *Nashville:* his only stipulation was that "someone should die at the end." But because Altman relies so heavily on improvisation, the script was really a group effort by the entire cast and crew, under the supervision of the director. Altman encouraged his performers to change or invent their own dialogue, and to add bits from their own personal backgrounds to the characters they were playing. Lengthy rehearsals took place before the filming of each scene so that everybody would have a chance to work out these details for himself or herself. *Nashville* was filmed in sequence, so that the performers would have a clear feeling for the progression of events. (In contrast, the scenes for most movies are shot in whatever order is most convenient for making use of the sets, locations, and stars.)

Most members of the cast of *Nashville* relished the chance of working in such an atmosphere of freedom and experimentation. "He's such an extraordinary director," says Tomlin, "yet he was never intimidating. He never made me feel afraid of expressing something, even though this was only my first movie and he was the biggest director in Hollywood. He had such faith in you that you just had to work that much harder to justify his faith."

Altman especially encouraged his cast to write the lyrics for the songs they sing in the film. Tomlin fans should take note that Lily is credited for writing the words to "Yes I do," a gospel number which she and a choir perform during the opening credits. Because of this song she was made a member of ASCAP, the American Society of Composers, Authors, and Publishers.

When *Nashville* was released in June 1975, it was wildly praised (and often overpraised) by nearly every reviewer. Pauline Kael, writing for *The New Yorker*, called it "the funniest epic vision of America ever to reach the screen. . . . I've never before seen a movie I loved in quite this way." Pulling out all the stops, *Newsweek* said that "*Nashville* is everything a work of social art ought to be but seldom is—immensely moving yet terribly funny, chastening yet ultimately exhilirating. It is also that rarest thing in contemporary movies—a work of art that promises to be hugely popular."

The critics were ecstatic not only about Robert Altman, but about Lily Tomlin as well. In *Time* Jay Cocks wrote, "Of all the reasons for which *Nashville* will be remembered, not the least is the movie debut of Lily Tomlin, extraordinary in the role of an upper–middle-class suburban wife who sings with a black gospel group. Anyone who knows Tomlin's particularly shrewd and quirky kind of comedy from television will not be surprised that her same skills come through here. . . . She is a major actress."

Tomlin's performance was nominated for but didn't win an Oscar, although she was named as "Best Supporting Actress" by the New York Film Critics. It was an award that was richly deserved, for Tomlin's portrayal of Linnea is unmistakably believable and poignant. She underplays throughout and her acting is refreshingly free of clichés.

"My *Nashville* lady could have been played in a lot of ways," Lily explains. "It seemed to me that she had so much going for her in the script, it was enough to begin on her just by thinking of her as a nice person, as human. I felt that in *Nashville* I could have handled just about any of those women, but if Bob

Altman wanted me to do the one I was least likely for, the only non-comedic role—okay, then maybe he knew something about me I didn't. I don't separate serious from funny in my head, or call one piece comedic, another dramatic. To me, it's all mixed together, like life."

As Tomlin plays her, Linnea is the warmest, most sympathetic person in the movie. She is just about the only character who truly cares about other people and is considerate of their feelings. Linnea is an outsider in Nashville, unimpressed by the glamour of show biz. She is happiest when she can be with her two children, who are both deaf. Sadly, her husband, Delbert Reese, who is Haven Hamilton's lawyer, seems to take no notice of her and the children. In an especially touching scene we see Linnea patiently drawing the story from her son of how well he is doing in a swimming class. Delbert (solidly played by Ned Beatty) can only stand by uneasily and watch them, because he's never bothered to learn sign language. (Tomlin took courses in signing so that she would be totally authentic in this scene.)

Dissatisfied with her marriage, Linnea is attracted to a handsome young folksinger, Tom Frank (Keith Carradine). She rejects his advances for a while, hanging up on him when he calls her. Against her better judgment, she finally acquiesces to his invitation to hear him sing at a local night spot. When she comes in and sits down at a table near the bar, Tom notices her and says to the audience, "I'm going to dedicate this to someone kind of special who just might be here tonight." Then he begins singing a bittersweet love song entitled, "I'm Easy." What follows is a wonder-fully moving sequence, which is Tomlin's best moment in the picture.

Three women are present in the audience on this night who have recently gone to bed with Tom. As he plays "I'm Easy," we can see that each of them believes that she is the special one he is singing to. But the viewer can tell that the song is actually for Linnea, who sits in the back, flattered yet still hesitant. Her faint smile, her confused expression, and her sad, longing eyes tell a story that would make any dialogue at this point totally superfluous. It's a heartbreaking moment. As Henry Gibson says, "I will always cherish the bar scene when Lily listens to Keith Carradine. The look on her face—a combination of love for this rock singer and guilt for the adultery she knew would take place—why, it just tears you."

Even sadder is the next scene between Linnea and Tom. For him, it's clear that the interest was mainly in adding another conquest to his long list. (Usually surrounded by groupies who throw themselves at him, it must have been quite a challenge for Tom to see if he could actually seduce someone as upright as Linnea.) Before she has left his motel room, he is already calling another woman.

Part of the reason we feel so much for Linnea is that the other characters in *Nashville* are so shallow and unsympathetic. People are constantly squabbling over petty differences, usually involving money or status. Altman seems to take the view that human relationships are almost always doomed to be meaningless and empty. No one is truly able to communicate with anyone else; instead people use one another to further their own schemes.

Yet many of the other characters in the movie are very colorful, and it's usually entertaining to watch how they go about handling (and mishandling) their lives. Ronee Blakley is fine as Barbara Jean. And she is just about the only member of the cast who can sing passably well: most of the others, unfortunately, can't sing a lick. Blakley wrote most of the touching scene in which her character's mind wanders during a performance. She starts babbling on about some incident from her childhood, and her ever-fickle fans immediately turn against her, booing with no consideration for her delicate state of mind and all the problems she's been facing.

Though his voice is as mellifluous as an old bullfrog's, Henry Gibson is very amusing as Haven Hamilton: he is arrogant in a way that only very short men can be. He treats his subordinates with contempt. He's fond of wearing white cowboy outfits and ridiculous toupees. And his songs either dispense cheap sentiment or jingoism. For example, one song proclaims that "we must be doin' somethin' right to last two hundred years." In another one Hamilton twangs, "I can't leave my wife, and there's three reasons why—there's Jimmy, there's Cathy, there's sweet Loreli. For the sake of the children, we must say goodbye."

Hamilton's songs are so godawful they're funny. But at the same time this is the very sort of thing that is most troubling about *Nashville*: the filmmakers have set up some very easy targets here. Someone like

Haven Hamilton is obviously laughable, but is this supposed to be a comment on the better country singers who are sincerely trying to sing about their own experiences? What about, say, Hank Williams, or Patsy Cline or Waylon Jennings? There's a certain mean-spiritedness in *Nashville*. We have the sense, much of the time, that the filmmaker looks down on the characters, that he feels superior to the poor benighted fools who actually enjoy country music and are moved by it. The ultimate insult comes in the closing scenes, after the assassination. Nashville folk are apparently so insensitive that they can see their idol brutally murdered—and yet a few minutes later be found singing cheerfully. Significantly, the only character who reacts in a humane way is Linnea, whom we see looking devastated and confused, unable to join in the singing.

Yet for all the limitations of Altman's misanthropic point of view, *Nashville* has many rewards to offer the viewer. Above all, there is the cast. It's difficult to think of another film that features so many outstanding performances. Altman certainly has an unusual method of making a film—he sees himself as part director/part summer-camp counselor—and he often liberates performers to go beyond anything they've done in the past. And Altman is brilliant at casting: virtually everyone in *Nashville* was cast against type, yet with surprisingly effective results. Another good point about the film is that it is very pleasant to look at, despite its sardonic message. Altman and his cinematographer, Paul Lohmann, have a clear preference for cool, poster-bright colors. The shooting style of the film includes many short takes, and with all the quick cutting there's an impressionistic and spontaneous feeling to what happens in *Nashville*.

Despite her newfound acclaim in the movies, Tomlin did not give up her appearances on television after she made *Nashville*. Her next TV special was *People*, a ninety-minute pilot that was shown on NBC on August 28, 1976. It was distinctly different from her previous efforts. Instead of having the more familiar format of a TV variety show, *People* was an attempt to produce a video version of the popular magazine about celebrities that is published by Time, Inc. Jane Wagner was hired as the creator, writer, and executive producer of the show. It came as no surprise to anybody that she turned immediately to Tomlin. The idea was that Lily would be the hostess and interviewer for this fast-paced look at people in the news.

Loretta Lynn, Dick Cavett, and Louise Lasser are among those featured in the pilot for *People*. In the profile of Lasser, she tells Tomlin, "The thing I like about your comedy—it's not funny." Another segment features Tomlin playing with Koko, a four-year-old gorilla with a vocabulary in sign language of three hundred words. Viewers are also treated to a glimpse of Tomlin doing her act at a Boston concert. She tells the audience, "Every time I see a 'Yield' sign in the road, I feel sexually threatened."

Alas, this was the first and last episode of *People*, even though reviewers had some nice words for it. *The New York Times* said, "Miss Tomlin is sensational," and the *Christian Science Monitor* said, "Lily

Tomlin's *People* is a soft-edged satirical gem that constitutes a national treasure. . . . Unfailingly, she gets to the essence of the people she is portraying or interviewing."

Tomlin won another Emmy for the next show she was involved with, *The Paul Simon Special,* which was broadcast by NBC on December 8, 1977. Actually, her role in this effort was pretty small. But since she was credited as one of the writers, she became a winner of the 1977–78 Emmy for "Best writing for a comedy, variety, or music special." Although her other Emmies have certainly all been well deserved, her award for *The Paul Simon Special* was something of a fluke. What's excellent about this show is the music, not the comedy. Paul Simon sings some of his most tuneful songs from the seventies, and best of all is his captivating duet with Art Garfunkel on a sixties' song, "Old Friends."

Lorne Michaels, who produced *The Paul Simon Special,* came up with the format: the making of a special about Paul Simon. Charles Grodin plays a TV producer who tries to find a way to make his low-keyed, easygoing star more exciting. Simon gives a concert at which the audience response is lukewarm, so Grodin proposes intercutting footage of an enthusiastic crowd applauding feverishly. Simon is not amused.

Lily comes on near the end of the show. She tries to cheer up Simon, who is depressed about how his special seems to be turning out. Says Lily, "Yeah, but everyone feels like that sometimes. And when things do come together, it's almost magical. Sometimes the biggest failure turns out to be the biggest success. You

can't always tell how it's going to come out . . . Mitch
Miller is a classic example. He went on TV with 'Sing
Along with Mitch,' wasn't that a great idea? But it
didn't happen right away. In the beginning he used to
go door-to-door; he'd do 'Sing Along with You.' Then
someone said to him, 'Mitch, you'll exhaust yourself.'
So you see, you never know.''

Tomlin's next movie performance, in *The Late
Show* (1977), was in its own way every bit as fine as
her contribution to *Nashville*. On the strength of her
outstanding work in her first movie, she was able to
get top billing opposite Art Carney in her second. *The
Late Show*, which was written and directed by Robert
Benton and produced by Robert Altman, tells about
the rather offbeat adventures of an aging Los Angeles
private eye, Ira Wells (Carney), and his client, Margo
(Tomlin).

The Late Show is very much in the tradition of
the hard-boiled detective films of the forties, such as
The Maltese Falcon and *The Big Sleep*. The rejuvenat-
ing twist is that the detective is no longer Humphrey
Bogart in his prime, but is instead Art Carney, who
walks with a limp, wears a hearing aid, and could
stand to lose fifty pounds. The woman in the case is
not a dangerous femme fatale out of Dashiell Hammett
or Raymond Chandler: on the contrary, Margo is an
endearingly dizzy kook.

The mystery begins when a former partner of
Ira's, Harry Regan, shows up one day with a bullet in
his stomach. Regan dies without naming his murderer
and Ira vows to discover who was responsible for the
crime. At Regan's funeral, Ira is approached by Margo,

who wants to hire him to find her kidnapped cat. As any fan of murder mysteries would quickly guess, these two crimes turn out to be connected, although Ira Wells's detective skills (and his ailing body) are taxed to the limit as he and Margo go about unraveling the case.

Tomlin gives one of her most resourceful performances in *The Late Show*. Margo is a difficult character to handle effectively because the movie depends on audiences remaining sympathetic to her even though many of her ideas are totally off the wall. Margo is a chattering, nutty person who has dabbled in just about every fad that has come along. She's smoked a little too much grass. She takes an interest in astrology. When she doesn't like someone, she is fond of saying, "He is not a truly evolved person." Margo is the epitome of Southern Californian rootlessness. She came to Los Angeles to become an actress, but now, in her thirties, she really doesn't know what she wants out of life. She just drifts along, and tries to adapt herself to whichever way the wind happens to be blowing.

Tomlin says: "If I had come to California and stayed here at the beginning of my career, I might have ended up like Margo. I've known people like her, girls who don't make it as actresses and end up trying to be dress designers, or managers of other people's careers, or maybe dealing a little dope. Specifically, I did have a friend who was always going to manage some singer or actress, but never did.

"The thing about Margo is that I wanted her to come across as a drifter, yet someone who still has a

certain innocence, a belief that life is worth something. She's someone who is still in there *believing*,
and that's what I like about her."

The relationship of Margo and Ira is what *The
Late Show* is all about. The garish minor characters
and the labyrinthian plot exist mainly as an excuse to
bring these two very different people together. Ira is a
straight, proud man who sees himself as a defender of
honest principles and human decency. He is a highly
rational, tough-minded individual who doesn't quite
know how to react to somebody with the laid-back
mentality of Margo. Ira Wells has known better days
and less seedy neighborhoods, but he is not the sort of
guy to complain about his situation. He does have a
sense of humor, albeit a dry one, as he observes how
the world around him has changed. It pleases him no
end when he gets a chance to outwit men younger
than himself. On one occasion a young guy says to
him suspiciously, "You look kind of old to be a cop."
And Ira replies, "Don't worry—this is just a disguise."

Art Carney gives a winning performance as Ira
Wells; we're moved by his portrayal of a man of honor
living in a dishonorable world. Lily had always
looked up to Carney as one of her idols. "What an exciting opportunity *The Late Show* became," says Lily.
"I'd watched Art Carney for years on 'The Honey-
mooners.' So when I played a scene opposite him
there was all the history and excitement of someone
who had preceded me, someone I'd associated with
the history of comedy."

Best of all their moments together in *The Late
Show* is the scene in which Margo suggests to Ira that

they should live together. She's become exhilarated at how much she enjoys working with him. "I feel just like Nick and Nora, you know, from *The Thin Man*," she says. And she starts imagining a whole new life for them; she could be his new partner. She mentions that the apartment next door to hers is vacant, and he could move in. Ira thanks her, but says he has always been a loner and likes it that way. And then Margo tries to pretend it was all a joke, that she was just kidding. "Look, Ira, I don't want you to overinterpret what I was saying—it was just something to do, you know. It was an exciting kind of thing tonight, and I just got carried away with it." It's marvelous to watch Tomlin as she manages somehow to cry and laugh at the same time.

The Late Show was one of the "sleeper" hits of 1977. Made on a relatively modest budget and not heralded by much publicity, the film nevertheless was popular with critics and audiences alike. In the *New York Post*, Frank Rich called *The Late Show* "the first American movie of the year that's worth seeing and worth talking about."

Once again, the praise for Tomlin was virtually unanimous. Richard Schickel commented in *Time*, "Her impersonation . . . is just about perfect. So is the slow believable way she allows Carney's realism to win her over." In the *New Republic* Stanley Kauffmann wrote, "Tomlin is lovely. She has an instinct for truth which she handles unsententiously. Easily and delicately she creates this Hollywood nut whirling continually in a flurry of impulses as self-protection for central insecurity."

Because of *Nashville* and *The Late Show,* Tomlin began getting a great many offers for parts in films. But she turned down almost all of them. She explained in a 1975 interview: "I'd like to do more movies, but I want to do them the way I do TV specials—being responsible for the project. Unless I'm working with an Altman, someone I truly admire as an artist, I'm not too interested in just getting parts, being a body that someone uses in a film. I just like to do my own work, and I'm happy to say that I have an innocence, a belief that you can do it your way, that you don't have to play the game."

That she has always maintained such high standards is certainly an admirable trait of Lily's. Yet many of her fans feel that she has been a bit too choosy in selecting her movie roles. Not that she should grab anything that comes along, but many of us feel that we have been deprived of some of the fine character roles that she might have done. It's quite a tribute to the excellence of her performances in *Nashville* and *The Late Show* that she leaves us wanting to see more of her.

CHAPTER 7

APPEARING NITELY

By 1977 Lily Tomlin had had a major triumph in nearly every medium of entertainment. She'd won three Emmies for her TV specials and a Grammy for one of her records. She'd been nominated for an Academy Award for her first role in a movie, and she'd starred in the top-rated show on television. She had also performed at Carnegie Hall and before the British Royal Family. The only thing missing from Lily's résumé was that she hadn't yet been the star of a hit show on Broadway. Naturally, she was determined to fill this gap. (Lily hasn't yet perfected an act on the trapeze, but apart from that there are few other types of performances she hasn't attempted.)

After some tryout runs in Boston, Chicago, and San Francisco, Tomlin brought her first play, *Appearing Nitely*, to Broadway on March 24, 1977. This one-woman revue, which she co-wrote with Jane Wagner, was by far the biggest undertaking of her career up to that time. It wasn't merely an extended stand-up routine, but a carefully paced and well-structured piece of material. In *Appearing Nitely* she played fifteen different characters—including a few of her old favorites, such as Ernestine and Mrs. Beasley, and some new ones, such as Glenna, "a child of the sixties."

"My instincts tell me now's the time to do it," Lily told one reporter just before the Broadway premiere of *Appearing Nitely*. "But I'm still scared stiff."

Most of the material for the show had been tested as part of Tomlin's nightclub act at The Ice House in Pasadena and The Boarding House in San Francisco. Lily considers the audiences at those clubs to have been her collaborators in the development of *Appearing Nitely*: "I tried to work with them in a way that's different from other comedians. I didn't want the people to just sit back passively and look at me from some great distance, as if I were on a movie screen, or something. I wanted to bring them into the process." She recalls that, "At The Boarding House, I developed Crystal, my militant quadriplegic, and Tess, the eccentric shopping bag lady, and Rick, my first male character."

Tomlin and Wagner kept revising the play not only up until it opened on Broadway, but right through its New York run and afterward, when it toured other cities. Tomlin says she tried to keep the same comfortable feelings between her and the audiences regardless of whether she was in a small club or in the Biltmore Theater in New York. "No matter who I'm working in front of, if I believe in a character or a piece, I'll stick with it until it feels good—to me.

Audience response isn't my first criterion. Oh, you can do all kinds of easy stuff you know they'll respond to, but that does not mean that an audience and I have really communed, shared something. If they allow me to get away with easy junk, and I allow them to get by with that, then they don't leave with anything to think about. We haven't really taken care of each other, you know?"

Lily's intention with *Appearing Nitely* was to create a show that would have a more meaningful effect on people than most humor, which kills time pleasantly and leaves audiences the same as they were before the performance. "There has to be humanity and real character," she explains, "so that when it's over, you're better for it. You come away with something."

Audiences responded warmly to the show wherever it was performed, and the critics were almost unanimously favorable. *Appearing Nitely* was originally scheduled to run only four weeks on Broadway, but the show was extended to eight, then to twelve weeks. Tomlin could have continued to appear in New York for much longer—the theater was regularly sold out—but she wanted to get on with a national tour.

Those fans who lined up in the cold for tickets on the day the box office opened in New York got a special treat when Lily herself came out to greet them. In character as Mrs. Beasley, she wore a Red Cross uniform and handed out donuts and hot coffee. "Mrs. Beasley" had words of cheer for everyone, but she firmly denied knowing anything about Lily Tomlin. "I am a real person like yourself," she told her fans. "I personally have never met Lily and I don't know why that woman is taking my likeness."

One of the most impressive features of *Appearing Nitely* was the evidence it provided of Tomlin's growth as a comedienne. Most entertainers are content to coast along on their past successes, giving audiences more of whatever made them famous. Tomlin could have stuck exclusively with her "sure-fire" characters from "Laugh-In." Indeed, she probably could have been the star of her own variety series or sitcom by the late seventies, had she been willing to compromise her material in order to please network executives. But instead of taking the easiest path, she pushed herself to meet new challenges, such as those offered by *Appearing Nitely*.

The show was more demanding for Tomlin, both as a performer and as a writer, than any of her previous efforts. In the end she proved fully capable of rising to the occasion: *Appearing Nitely* became one of the best things she's ever done. The show features a group of characters who range the spectrum of types. They vary widely in age, social position, education, sophistication, and common sense. Yet all seem equally real and believable when Lily portrays them.

In *Appearing Nitely* there is no scenery, there are virtually no props, and no one else is on the stage— just Lily, in a gray blouse and black slacks. But that is more than enough. She becomes the entire cast, in a virtuosic display of comic acting. Lily proved with *Appearing Nitely* that her talent is equal to the demands of the theater, which are much greater than those of movies and television, where performers have the chance to do multiple takes of even the shortest scenes. Most of those actors who are able to be convincing when they portray one character for thirty seconds would be completely out of their depth if they tried to do what Tomlin does. Amazingly, Lily Tomlin is able, all by herself on a bare stage, to hold an audience's attention for over two hours.

Her performance is not only a histrionic feat, but also something of an athletic one, as anybody will attest to who has seen the amount of energy she puts into her work. Yet Lily says she has never followed any special regimen of diet and exercise, other than "eating healthy and staying active." (Two hours of performing every night on a Broadway stage should qualify as an activity.) "I've always been very strong, very athletic," she explains. "I've always been a fighter. I'm not afraid of my body. Most women don't know how to use their bodies. There's something so pathetic about that." Lily adds, "I used to set physical obstacles for myself. I'd dive for rings in the pool. I'd keep diving and diving, picking up more each time. I'd never swim just to swim."

In addition to her physical stamina, Tomlin possesses a remarkable sense of comic timing and the ability to find the right nuances to bring a character to life. Whether it's the way an irritated husband rustles his newspaper or the way in which a stoned teenager brushes the hair out of her eyes, Tomlin is firmly in command of the appropriate details of gestures and expression. She also has a fine ear for American dialects; she's able to reproduce the various ways that people actually talk, not just how they sound in the movies or on TV.

Tomlin is at her most astonishing when she switches from one character to another in the same scene, such as in the sketch from *Appearing Nitely* about Lud and Marie, a middle-aged couple, and their daughter. We really get the impression that all three of them are up there on the stage together.

The writing, much of it Jane Wagner's, is usually every bit as perceptive as Tomlin's acting. (The only significant weakness of *Appearing Nitely* is that Tomlin and Wagner have a tendency to overindulge their fondness for one-liners: sometimes we're all too aware that the characters have some mighty clever writers to supply lines for them.) What's outstanding about most of the script is that it reveals a sharp eye—and ear—for details. *Appearing Nitely* is made up of a large number of minute social observations. For instance, in a scene about a second-grader who idolizes her teacher, the girl says, "One day when I should have been coloring Lake Michigan blue I looked up and saw Miss Sweeney . . ." Now, that's a great touch—"coloring Lake Michigan blue"—because it's something a child might say but most adults wouldn't think of.

Frequently in *Appearing Nitely* there are moments that show the authors to be people who have done an astute job of scrutinizing the American scene. Tomlin often portrays people who may seem to be victims of their own ordinariness. Typically, most of her characters are not of the type who occupy lofty positions in society. They're usually telephone operators or waitresses or maybe shy schoolgirls. Quite a few of the characters in *Appearing Nitely* would have to be described as misfits. Some of them, like Tess and Crystal, are virtual outcasts, without friends or relatives.

Yet no matter how down-and-out the characters are, Lily portrays them with such sympathy that she brings out whatever is best in them. One thing most of her characters have in common is that they are usually outspoken and independent-minded. Crystal is a quadriplegic who defines her affliction as a sign of her superiority to "all you walkies." Tess, the shopping bag lady, claims she prefers living on the streets to living in the comforts of a home.

Lily admits to being fascinated by eccentric people, both in real life and in her work: "Aren't we all attracted not to the predictable people who always fit in, but to the one person in a crowd who's out of sync, and yet has no problem being that way? The person who doesn't do what we're all supposed to do, yet is perfectly confident in nonconformity? Her eccentricities are *your* problem, not hers! In all these characters I look for that essence. I had to work hard for that in Tess."

This comment is revealing in several ways. Lily is describing those people she loves to portray, but she's also describing herself. She is by no means an outcast, but definitely is someone who from an early age was happy to be a nonconformist. Lily has always been "out of sync," and proud of it.

For those who love eccentrics, Tess is undoubtedly a favorite character in *Appearing Nitely*. Her habits are indeed peculiar: she rifles through every garbage can she passes, she sells potholders on busy street corners, and she talks to little men from outer space. This crazy but gallant woman has only recently been released from a mental hospital. "How ya doin'? I just got out," she yells at the people she encounters on the street. "Did ya miss me? You wanna buy a potholder? I made these potholders when I was inside, to keep from goin' bats. I didn't like it in there, but boy I don't like it out here either. The reason I got in is somebody told 'em that I think I'm God . . . But I didn't say I *was* God, I said I *seen* God. Boy, they don't like people seein' things they can't see!"

Crystal, the militant quadriplegic, is confined to a wheelchair, yet she says she intends to go to Big Sur in California, where she will take up hang-gliding. Her wheelchair is nicknamed the "Iron Duchess," and is even equipped with a CB radio, on which she broadcasts insults to trunk drivers. In *Appearing Nitely* Crystal tells the audience about some of her supposed adventures while traveling across the country: "At a carnival outside Decatur, a kid climbs into my lap and asks, 'Are you a ride?' I said, 'I'm probably the best ride here.'"

Mrs. Beasley is wonderfully wholesome and earnest during her appearances in the play. In one bit she does a kind of parody of the typical public service announcements we've all heard on television. In a grave voice she tells the audience, "Most of us are aware of our diminishing supply of natural resources. But did you know that we are also running out of *unnatural* resources? . . . This is a genuine synthetic crisis. Trees can be grown, but with plastics you have to start from scratch." Mrs. Beasley worries that if nothing is done, there will be a panic for plastics, and "Greedy people will start hoarding baggies, shower curtains, Astroturf, and leisure suits." Moreover, "Unless we stop squandering and start conserving our unnatural resources, there will be an end to civilization as we know it . . . Studies have shown that over two-thirds of TV game show items are made of some form of plastic."

Ernestine shows up briefly in *Appearing Nitely*, to do a commercial for the telephone company. "We realize that every so often your phone goes out of order," she says. "And maybe you get charged for a call you didn't make. We don't care . . . We have a matrix of multimillion-dollar space age technology that is so sophisticated even we can't control it. The next time you want to complain about your phone service, try using two Dixie cups and a string."

Another memorable Tomlin impersonation from the play is that of Rick, the bar cruiser. He swaggers around and tries to pick up girls with corny come-on lines that never seem to work. He goes up to one "chick" and says, "I promised my buddy there he could have first crack at you . . . Hey, where're you going? . . . I just can't find a woman these days who doesn't have a sex problem." Finally, he decides to give up singles bars for supermarkets, because only some women drink, but "they all gotta eat." It would have been easy for Tomlin simply to have demolished Rick, exposing him as a total boor. Yet she lets us see the humanity that's lurking (far) beneath the macho surface of the character. The fact is that Rick is quite nervous about meeting women, and is genuinely puzzled about why he doesn't seem to appeal to them. His wife left him not long ago and he's actually a rather pathetic figure, more lonely than aggressive and more ignorant than crass.

The sketch about the second-grader and her crush on Miss Sweeney is definitely a highlight of the play. Lily captures some of those experiences from childhood that grown-ups usually try to forget. Little Lily tells of the anguish she felt one day in school when she pronounced the "s" in the word "island" while reading aloud. "You think you're okay and then something comes along like *is*-land, and then you know you're nothing special," she says.

The sketch about Glenna, "a child of the sixties," is a comic gem. In a Valley Girl accent, her lines include a gold mine of teenage slang from twenty years ago. "What's your sign?" she asks someone she's just met. "I knew it! Pisces just blow me away." Or after getting stoned she'll say, "Where's a mirror? I want to watch my pupils dilate . . . Wow, TV is soooo heavy—no, man, don't turn it on." Glenna's parents want to know what is going on behind her closed door, but she just tells them, "The door is locked because we are meditating. Mother, if you don't trust me, how am I ever going to trust myself?" At a protest rally Glenna later says to one of her friends, "I know all about imperialism and fascism from my parents."

In this twenty-minute sequence, Tomlin capsulizes the whole era of the sixties and early seventies through the viewpoint of Glenna. By the end of the sketch, she has become a feminist and has gotten married to a young lawyer who is "working to change the system from within." (In Tomlin's next play, *The Search for Signs of Intelligent Life in the Universe*, the story of Lyn is to a considerable extent a continuation of the story of Glenna. *The Search for Signs* picks up the character in the early seventies, around the time that *Appearing Nitely* leaves off.)

At several points in *Appearing Nitely* Tomlin speaks directly to the audience: at these moments she addresses some of the things in our society that make her uneasy. "I worry," she says, "that the person who thought up Muzak may be thinking up something else." Furthermore, "I worry about kids today. Because of the sexual revolution they're going to grow up and never know what dirty means." And, "Why is it we are always hearing about the tragic cases of too much, too soon? What about the rest of us? Too little, too late." Lily also wonders, "If truth is beauty, how come no one has her hair done at the library?" In these sections of *Appearing Nitely* Lily comes up with dozens of witty—and often thought-provoking—lines.

From New York, the show moved on to Philadelphia, Washington, and other cities. *Appearing Nitely* wound up grossing about $2 million in 1977 alone. Tomlin would occasionally remount it during the next six years, right up until the time she began doing *The Search for Signs*.

Tomlin was given a special Tony Award in 1977 for her work in *Appearing Nitely*. And for those fans who weren't able to see her in person, in late 1977 she released a recording of the show, entitled *Lily Tomlin: On Stage*. There are some interesting differences between the album, which was "conceived and produced" by Jane Wagner, and the original version of the play. *Lily Tomlin: On Stage* is designed to be a mock "night on Broadway." The exaggeratedly mellifluous baritone voice of "Mr. Theater-Goer" opens the album "from a little theater off Broadway and Forty-seventh Street." The campy narrator invites us to join him as he tells us, "The crowd is elegantly dressed. What a glamorous evening!" Before he can take his seat he encounters Tess, who says, "My pockets may be empty but my shopping bag is full." After the play Tess gets into Lily Tomlin's cab, and warns her about the "UFO guy."

Reviewers of the play and the album were unrestrained in their gushing praise for Lily. The word "genius" was frequently used to describe her. Clive Barnes, in his review for *The New York Times*, said: "Her talent is astonishing. . . . She is limitless. She takes an audience by the hand and disconcertingly leads it up to a mirror, and then giggles. Miss Tomlin is not a comic attitude, she is more of a comic conscience." Jack Kroll, writing for *Newsweek*, called Tomlin's play "a total assault on her audiences' sensibility—their minds, their hearts, their funny bones. There was always that extra dimension to Lily Tomlin's comedy. But watching her put the new show together, it's clear that she's reached the point where laughter is simply the final confirmation of the penetration of her insights."

Besides being praised to the skies by nearly every critic, Lily was the subject of dozens of feature articles and profiles in the leading national magazines, including a cover story for the March 28, 1977 issue of *Time*. All this publicity brought her more attention than she had ever received. After all, her work in *Nashville* and on "Laugh-In" had been as a member of an ensemble of performers. Even in her TV specials she had shared the limelight with Richard Pryor or other comedians. With *Appearing Nitely*, however, the focus was on Lily alone. The acclaim was extraordinary, as the critics were searching their dictionaries for every complimentary adjective they could find. But when she appeared in her next important project, they would be describing it in words of a very different kind.

CHAPTER 8

A MOMENT
TO FORGET

Ever since Tomlin became famous for her characterizations on "Laugh-In," she had experienced
nothing but one success after another. TV specials,
movies, records, concerts, a Broadway show—all had
made money and were favorably reviewed. She was so
much the darling of the press, that it wouldn't have
been surprising if, when she was finally involved in
something less than first-rate, they were waiting ea-
gerly to knock her off her pedestal. Which was exactly
what happened with *Moment by Moment*, a 1978 film
in which she and John Travolta were cast in the starring roles.

Written and directed by Jane Wagner, *Moment by
Moment* is about a love affair between a middle-aged
woman from Beverly Hills, named Trisha, and a
young street punk, named Strip (after Sunset Strip).
An important part of Wagner's point in making the
film was to break down sexual stereotypes: Tomlin's
character is the one who's most interested in sex and

the Travolta character is the one who most needs to be reassured that he is lovable. Yet this was the very aspect of the picture that was criticized the most mercilessly by the press.

The notices weren't merely unfavorable, they were downright venomous. In *New York* David Denby suggested that *Moment by Moment* was destined to be cherished by "future generations of movie trash-lovers." And in the opinion of Frank Rich, the reviewer for *Time*, it "may some day occupy a hallowed place in the pantheon of high camp." He fixed the blame primarily on the screenplay, which, according to Rich, "switches tone from scene to scene almost without warning. Embarrassingly enough, the sentimental moments are far funnier than Wagner's wisecracks about southern California mores. The suds are soon indistinguishable from the froth, and *Moment by Moment* becomes a tidal wave of inanity. . . . Next to this film, *Grease* starts to look like *Citizen Kane*."

Most of the critics sounded positively blood-thirsty as they ripped apart virtually every aspect of the film, from the directing and acting to the cinematography and music. *Moment by Moment* acquired such a bad reputation that it was even listed in *The Golden Turkey Awards*, Harry and Michael Medved's book on the worst films of all time. Before *Heaven's Gate* and *Ishtar* were released, *Moment by Moment* was looked on by the film industry as one of the standards against which box-office failures could be measured.

What was especially surprising was that even Tomlin's performance was savaged. She had always

been considered as an actress who was virtually inca-
pable of making a false move, yet her portrayal of Trisha was called "wooden" and "unbelievable." The
critic for *Newsweek* described her as "a frozen mask
under which one feels only subterranean rumblings of
unexplained rage. It is amazing that Wagner . . . has
given her so little to work with. Tomlin has always
been a master at projecting herself into socially mar-
ginal characters, but confronted with an 'Establishment' woman, her sympathetic imagination deserts
her. Even the most underdeveloped Beverly Hills
housewife has *some* personality."

We may feel that there is even a touch of glee in
the relentless disapproval of some of the critics. In
New York David Denby wrote that Tomlin was "acting
in a style so pale, tight, and uncommunicative that
she looked like a thirteen-year-old gritting her teeth
through a summer-camp production of *Come Back,
Little Sheba*."

There was no consolation, either, when the box-
office returns came in, for *Moment by Moment* proved
to be the only Tomlin picture that was not popular
with audiences.

Most moviegoers might assume that *Moment by
Moment* was made with the idea of capitalizing on
Travolta's phenomenal popularity from *Saturday
Night Fever*. But this isn't so. When Kevin McCormick, the executive producer of *Moment by Moment*,
first approached Travolta with the idea for the project,
they were standing on the Verrazano Narrows Bridge
between Brooklyn and Staten Island, about to shoot
the well-known scene from *Saturday Night Fever*. Mc-

Cormick remembers that Travolta was ecstatic at the thought of working with Lily: "He said that Lily was the most important performer of the century. I think there may be a little hyperbole in that."

At this time Tomlin was doing *Appearing Nitely*, and McCormick first met with her and Jane Wagner backstage at the Biltmore Theater in New York. He showed them some early footage from *Saturday Night Fever*, and they were so impressed they quickly agreed to work with Travolta.

Tomlin and Travolta soon became fast friends, and they were often seen together off the set. In an interview with a *Newsweek* reporter in May 1978, Travolta said, "We're very much in tune." And Lily added, "I don't think of him as being younger. He's *appealing*. We feel like we knew each other in another time."

They were highly affectionate in public, holding hands and making flirtatious remarks. During one interview, Lily referred to him as "you millionaire cutie." On another occasion she said, "It's not hard to relate to him sexually. Maybe it's the image he's built up on-screen, but I was thinking on the plane, sitting next to him, that . . . he certainly is an object of desire."

In spite of all the flirting in public, what went on privately between them isn't all that clear. It's possible that Tomlin and Travolta's "relationship" was mainly designed to create more publicity for the film. And one can't help taking note that they were seen together socially only during the period just before and after the release of *Moment by Moment*.

Before the film was released, Tomlin and Travolta both believed that it would be something of a breakthrough in the way that men and women were depicted on the screen. In his 1978 *Playboy* interview Travolta said, "This may be a turning point in film, because you're seeing a man for the first time going through as much emotional change and coloration as women have in the past. . . . I really think the film can make a statement." In an interview with *The New York Times*, Travolta explained, "I'm hoping that men can say, 'If it's okay for that character and John Travolta to feel that, maybe it's okay for *me* to feel and express that, too.'"

Lily's hopes were nearly as high as Travolta's for *Moment by Moment*, and she also felt that filmgoers would be intrigued by characters who didn't follow the traditional sex roles. "Our movie is meant to be a romantic movie," Tomlin said in the same *Times* interview, "but I think it's much more realistic than those in which the man is more dominant and the female character, mostly conceived and written by men, is put in nonthreatening roles."

Those viewers who get the chance to see *Moment by Moment* today—which is not an easy task, for it isn't shown often and isn't available on videotape—will discover that the movie is neither as atrocious as the critics charged nor as inspiring as the filmmakers hoped. Instead, it's a fairly mediocre effort with some major flaws but a few good moments as well. No one could miss the fact that *Moment by Moment* was made with (too many?) noble intentions, which is surely part of the explanation for why the film was so fiercely attacked. Critics often feel that a dreadful but unpretentious movie, made only to cash in on a recent trend, isn't worth much attention. But with all its lofty aspirations, a film like Moment by Moment offers an inviting target.

The best scenes in the movie are the early ones in which we're introduced to the main characters. (It isn't until the love affair really blossoms that Moment by Moment runs into serious trouble.) Trisha is a woman who has become bored with her comfortable life in Beverly Hills. She has no job, her son is away at school, and her husband has taken up with a younger woman, so she has little left to fill up her time besides sunning herself at her Malibu beach house and petting her little white terrier. On a shopping trip to Rodeo Drive, Trisha encounters Strip. He is a drifter who ran away from home when he was fourteen and who has had dealings with some pretty unsavory characters: his best friend is Gregg, a drug pusher. Strip makes a series of attempts to pick Trisha up, but she is icy toward him. He starts hanging out around her beach house. In the beginning she feels he's just another punk, yet she eventually discovers that at heart he is really a very sweet kid who would never do harm to anyone. He is actually a much better person than most of her well-to-do friends.

Tomlin's portrayal of Trisha was attacked by reviewers for being "unemotional" and "deadpan," but this criticism is not at all deserved. She in fact conveys a quiet sense of gravity that is appropriate for the character: Trisha is a person who has been afraid of her own emotions. Her character is one of muted passions and frustrated hopes. It's actually a much more difficult part than that of, say, Trudy the shopping bag lady, with all of her obvious eccentricities. Performers are frequently lavished with praise for their more colorful portrayals, while their more subtle pieces of acting often go unnoticed by the press.

Tomlin explains that Trisha is "facing the numbing fact that the status quo she's maintained for years is basically empty. She's only invested in her husband's life. . . . Trisha is not so different from me that I cannot imagine common feelings and experiences. I've seen her in the shops in Beverly Hills. She is a bright, attractive woman who has gained money and status in her community but has lost something in exchange. Strip reminds her that she is closed off, that part of her life has stopped."

Travolta's performance is engagingly boyish, and he does a fine job of letting us see the vulnerability of his character. Those moviegoers who think of him as simply another "hunk" ought to take a look at *Moment by Moment*. The problem with his character is not due to Travolta's portrayal, but to the screenplay, which forces him to do and say things that aren't at all credible. In a way, Travolta—and Tomlin—did their jobs too well: their solid performances only serve to make the inadequacies of the script even more obvious. Strip is supposed to be a street kid, hardened by dealings with the underworld, yet the script calls for him to be a sweet boy with more sensitivity than Alan Alda and Woody Allen put together. Also, did the filmmakers *have* to use the name "Strip"? At several moments this inevitably provokes unintended laughter from audiences. When Strip and Trisha embrace, Lily's character is fond of smiling contentedly and saying, "Strip, oh, Strip." Only the most serious viewer can get through these scenes without noticing how ludicrous this sounds.

At the heart of the failure of Moment by Moment is the whole idea of reversing the sexual roles. Yes, it all sounds interesting, but the result is that we wind up with characters who behave completely unlike recognizable people from the real world. Instead, it is a feminist's fantasy of how she would like to see men reacting.

The heights (or depths?) of absurdity are reached in a scene in Trisha's Jacuzzi. She invites Strip to join her, and after he takes off his briefs and steps into the water with her, they have this conversation:

STRIP: I love you. I just thought you should know. Do you love me? I know you do. Just say it.

TRISHA: Strip . . .

STRIP: You don't love me?

TRISHA: Oh, Strip.

STRIP: Am I not good enough for you, is that it?

TRISHA: Oh no, Strip, that's just not true.

STRIP: I was good enough for you this morning, wasn't I. You loved me this morning, didn't you?

TRISHA: Yes.

STRIP: You just don't love me out of bed.

Soon afterward, we see Strip, now out of the water, doing more than his share of pouting. He cocks back his head, looks away from Trisha, then returns to face her, his eyes brimming with tears. He tells her, "Look, if you're not ready to commit to a meaningful relationship with me—one that could be very beautiful, very uplifting—it's over. Because I've had it with cheap sex. It leaves me feeling cheap." Trisha puts her arms around him, reassuring him that she does love him for himself and not just for his body. (After this sequence no doubts remain that Strip is the most sensitive man alive.)

Another clear intention of the film was to reverse the practice of using women as sex objects. Hundreds, if not thousands, of movies have been made with the idea of showing off the bodies of actresses as much as current standards would allow. In *Moment by Moment*, though, it's Travolta's body that is constantly displayed. He is often shown wearing the skimpiest of briefs, while Tomlin is usually fully dressed. We frequently see her looking at his body with undisguised admiration. Advertisements for the movie featured a shot in which Tomlin, clothed, and Travolta, apparently naked, are embracing passionately. What's more, she is shown lying on top of him.

As soon as the film was released in December 1978, it was obvious that *Moment by Moment* was going to be an out-and-out disaster, the first flops in the careers of both stars. Reviewers often took note of the fact that audiences were finding parts of the movie to be hilariously awful. When people at previews laughed at lines that weren't supposed to be funny, Tomlin, Travolta, and Wagner tried to defend the picture. "We're very proud of the film," Tomlin told one reporter. Kevin McCormick was even more blunt in his response to the criticism: "The overreaction is hilarious," he said. "People feel threatened. Everybody is pissed at Lily. They want something they recognize. Film comedy. They don't want real life. The character Lily plays is real life. . . . The humor in *Moment by Moment* is so gentle that audiences don't know what they're supposed to do. They don't know whether to laugh or not."

Verna Fields, an executive with Universal, the production company for the film, believes that the critics and the Hollywood establishment exaggerated the failure of the movie because it was directed by a woman. "To be honest," says Fields, "I don't think *Moment by Moment* would have been perceived as such a failure if it had been by a male director, or if it had been the story of a middle-aged man having an affair with a little cutie on the beach. Nobody ever talks about *Goin' South* being a major failure for Jack Nicholson. Nobody ever talks about Paul Newman and *The Drowning Pool*; it died, and they let it die. They wouldn't let *Moment by Moment* die. There were a lot of expectations, because the two stars were both very hot at the time, and it's very hard for a director to meet such expectations. Particularly a first-time director. Particularly a woman director. Women aren't allowed to fail, you see."

The hostile reactions to *Moment by Moment* had a shattering effect on Lily. Throughout most of 1979 she kept a low profile, perhaps in an attempt to avoid being asked about the movie. Even now she doesn't like to talk about it anymore than necessary. "Maybe I just didn't do a good job," she says. "But none of us were prepared for the vicious attacks that followed. It involved an enormous amount of pain. For a year I couldn't pick up a magazine without reading some new dirt."

Lily says that the experience also had the effect of making her a stronger person, better able to cope with the setbacks that inevitably befall anybody at one time or another. Although she probably took the disaster of *Moment by Moment* too much to heart, she usually manages to handle the peaks and valleys of success and misfortune quite well. She's certainly not allowed herself to fall into the traps that so many other celebrities have failed to avoid. For Lily, the solution to most any problem has always been to involve herself as intensely as possible in her work.

It was during this difficult period that Lily bought and redecorated a large, old, pink stucco house in the Los Feliz neighborhood of Los Angeles. She and Jane Wagner have lived there ever since. The place used to belong to W. C. Fields; it's an old-fashioned Hollywood mansion with twenty-seven rooms. Lily has a lovely garden, and there's also a pool—with Edith Ann's giant chair nearby. Pictures of movie stars from the thirties, forties, and fifties hang on many of the walls. Lily describes the place as "casual, airy, light, very feminine, a soft house."

Although her house must have cost her a pretty penny, Lily doesn't spend a great deal on luxury items. Unlike others from fairly poor backgrounds, she doesn't appear to have a taste for conspicuous consumption. She explains that she has little interest in expensive clothing or trendy restaurants. She doesn't fly first class, she says, "Because it would be an insult to my family and the life we've known."

According to her brother, Richard, "Lily's idea of a night on the town is to go to Hamburger Hamlet, have dinner, and then go back home and work." (Even a Spartan, it seems, might describe Lily's style of living as "spartan.") Says Richard, "You can go crazy at her house. The phone is ringing all the time, with writers or producers talking deals. Lily literally works around the clock. How she juggles everything I couldn't tell you. It's a madhouse half the time."

CHAPTER 9

LILY TOMLIN— MOVIE STAR

Still smarting from the blow she had received with *Moment by Moment*, Lily was extremely careful in selecting her next role, which, she hoped, would establish her as "a popular, bankable, nonthreatening performer. . . . I had to bide my time, make a few successful comedies." She chose well, and her next important project, *9 to 5* (1980), directed by Colin Higgins, turned out to be one of the best-attended movies of the eighties. (It brought in over $59 million in the U.S., which made it the second biggest box-office attraction of 1980; only *The Empire Strikes Back* did better business that year.) Female moviegoers, in particular, enjoyed this comedy of revenge in which three secretaries—played by Tomlin, Jane Fonda, and Dolly Parton—kidnap their relentlessly chauvinistic boss.

Lily was enthusiastic about making the picture from the time she was first asked by Jane Fonda to appear in it. The original idea for *9 to 5* was Fonda's, and she was also the president of the company, IPC Films, that produced it (from all reports, not an inconvenient position for an actress to hold).

Fonda recalls, "I had wanted to work with Lily ever since I had seen her onstage [in *Appearing Nitely*], and we'd been talking about doing a movie for a few years. . . . Then I thought—it's about time for a movie with *three* leading ladies."

Like Tomlin, Fonda had once been a secretary herself, and she was interested in making a film that captured some of the problems that working women encounter. During the seventies Fonda had often given speeches before groups of office workers, and she remembers being moved by their stories. "One group I spoke to in Milwaukee—the clerical workers couldn't use the elevators; they had to walk up the back stairs. Only male executives had a key to the front door. . . . The office structure also pits women against each other very viciously: older women versus young, black and brown versus white, pretty versus ugly, thin versus fat. It's important who dresses better than whom. The sexual tensions, the pay problems, the lack of promotion . . ."

"While researching *9 to 5*," remembers Bruce Gilbert, the producer of the film, "we spoke to many women and learned a great deal about the undercurrents of what goes on in big offices. We asked the women to tell us about their jobs and their complaints, and we found again and again that the major problem was in the area of self-respect. They feel that you can run an office without bosses, but not without secretaries. . . . At a certain point, we asked the women if they had ever fantasized about getting even with their bosses. That was like opening a floodgate. Suddenly, the most bizarre and funny stories started coming out, and it certainly reinforced our decision to do the film as a comedy."

Lily Tomlin was a natural choice to play a part in the movie. After all, she was best known for having created Ernestine, who had long been popular with office workers and who would undoubtedly sympathize with the plight of women like the three main characters in 9 to 5.

Tomlin says that because of her recent debacle, *Moment by Moment*, she was particularly anxious as filming began for 9 to 5. "When I first thought of the three of us [Fonda, Parton, and herself] together, I assumed *I* would be the one to fail. I even called the producer after the first few days of filming and said it was all right to replace me. But Jane was very supportive. And Dolly—well, she's so smart and savvy. She's aware of everything she does. Her acting is as natural to her as putting on her wig."

All three actresses say they were pleased to discover they could work together easily, without any friction, even though each of them was a big star in her own right. And they enjoyed being together off-camera as well as on-camera. Lily recalls, "Dolly and Jane and I got to be like junior high girlfriends— slumber parties, the whole bit."

Dolly Parton says, "Working with Jane and Lily was a great inspiration. Lily, I just love her. She's so creative. And her folks, of course, were from the

South, just like mine. We have a great communication between us."

One of the best things going for 9 to 5 is its setting. Anybody who has ever worked in an office must be aware of the rich potential for comedy in the backstabbing, favoritism, bureaucratic inefficiencies, and petty dictatorships that are universally found in businesses, whether they have ten employees or ten thousand. Colin Higgins (who also directed the picture) and Patricia Resnick wrote the script for 9 to 5, and they succeeded in capturing much of the potential for humor in a typical office situation.

The movie begins with the arrival of Judy Bernly (Fonda) on her first day of work as a secretary for a large corporation. Her supervisor is Violet Newstead (Tomlin), a super-efficient veteran employee who keeps getting passed over when promotions are made. Judy and Violet's boss, we soon learn, is Franklin Hart (played, hilariously, by Dabney Coleman), a paragon of bigotry, lechery, and a long list of other moral shortcomings.

Not surprisingly, Violet bristles whenever Hart's name comes up in conversation. It really irks her that she has to take orders from someone who is obviously not as good at his job as she is at hers. She tells Judy, "Mr. Hart was just made vice president. I've never seen anyone leapfrog so fast to the top in my life. And I have the bad back to prove it. I remember when he was just a management trainee. In fact, I'm the one who trained him."

When Hart meets Judy, his first response is, "You're a welcome addition, and a damn pretty one, too—if I might add. I mean that. You should see some of the crones that have been coming through here lately. Real pathetic. Right, Violet?'' (Needless to say, Violet is not amused by this remark.)

We next encounter Doralee Rhodes (Parton), a warm-hearted, buxom blonde who is Hart's personal secretary. She hates Hart just as much as Violet and Judy do, and there is a sequence in which we see that each of the three secretaries has fantasies of killing him. The Tomlin character's fantasy is the funniest: she plays Snow White in a delightful scene in which she poisons him with the help of some animated creatures drawn in a style highly reminiscent of Walt Disney. Her eyes twinkle with glee as she opens her ring and drops the poison into her boss's morning coffee.

The next day, Violet accidentally does put rat poison into Hart's coffee, and their fantasies appear to be coming true. Violet excitedly says to Judy, "I thought it was Skinny 'n' Sweet. Here, look at the box. They're absolutely identical . . . except for the skull and crossbones on the label." Eventually, the three secretaries wind up kidnapping their boss, blackmailing him—and convincing the rest of the company's employees that he is still on the job, even though Violet is the one who's actually running the department in his absence. With the women in charge, office productivity is higher than ever, and they institute a series of long-overdue reforms, such as day care and more flexible working hours.

Although 9 *to* 5 is entertaining most of the time, occasionally the plot becomes overcomplicated and some of the characters become more like cartoons than real people. Many of the jokes, too, are less than sparkling, but the principal actresses and actors all seem to be having a great time, and as a result 9 *to* 5 turns out to be a very likable movie.

Tomlin's performance is a strong one, and more subtle than most of what happens around her in the movie. Violet is the most sensible of the three main characters—and the funniest to watch, as Tomlin gets the most out of her lines by adeptly underplaying throughout the film. "I'm no fool," Violet says at one crucial moment. "I've killed the boss. You think they're not going to fire me for a thing like that?" What is most amusing about Violet is that viewers can see that around the edges of what appears to be a poker face there lurks the expression of a woman who is positively seething with rage at all the unfair treatment she has had to endure over the years. Whenever Hart makes another demeaning remark, her eyes narrow as she fights her impulse to say something appropriately nasty back to him.

A reason that the scenes between Violet and her boss work so well is the terrific performance of Dabney Coleman, who excels at portraying a man we love to hate. He plays Hart as the kind of a guy who could make J. R. Ewing look compassionate. And Hart is not above doing such tacky things as dropping pencils on the floor so that he can leer at Doralee as she gets down on her hands and knees, her ample cleavage exposed.

Coleman explains that he didn't have to do any research to play the role, "Because I grew up around those people. . . . Businessmen are not foreign to me.

My uncles, my relatives, the people I went to school with, are now those people. My father-in-law is an executive, and I was influenced by him and his cronies."

He adds, "It's a lot of fun . . . to play men who are evil and funny. There's usually a lot to grab ahold of, and you can get a strong reaction from the audience. I don't consider myself a leading man, and barring that, the bad guy parts are usually the best written." Coleman recalls that his next acting job after 9 to 5 was in On Golden Pond. In that movie he played "a levelheaded, suburban, nice substantial guy. . . . I liked the part, but it's tough for me to be a nice guy. It's really tough." (It seems a safe bet that he was not given much serious consideration for the lead in, say, Gandhi.)

Although there were some favorable notices, 9 to 5 was not quite as popular with critics as it was with audiences. For instance, David Ansen's review in Newsweek said, "Colin Higgins's movie is a disappointment. Not a fiasco, a disaster, or a scandal. But not as funny as it should have been, and not the trenchant office satire one was led to expect." Meanwhile, the critic for Maclean's magazine wrote, "9 to 5 is deliciously complicated and delicately spun out. The writing . . . has the fleeciness of a good farce and the aching serious undertone of a classic one. It's a return to the buoyant and artful screwball comedies of Howard Hawks and Preston Sturges."

Even those who disliked the film had nothing but good things to say about Tomlin's portrayal of Violet Newstead (which must have been a great relief to Lily after her poor notices for Moment by Moment).

"Tomlin is a crackerjack comic actress, even when the convection is stale," commented Richard Corliss in *Time*. David Denby, writing for *New York*, said, "Fonda can't make much of her role, but Tomlin is in top form." And the reviewer for the *San Francisco Examiner* was almost worshipful in his praise: "While Tomlin's on screen, God's in Her heaven."

The most common negative comments about the film were that the caricatures were too broad and the plot was highly improbable. The critic for the *New Leader* went so far as to say, "Feminists should be appalled by this comedy. . . . The problem with Hart is not that he is sexist and stupid, even in sexual matters. Any boss in a major corporation who behaved as he does would quickly be dragged into court. If *9 to 5* has a feminist message, it is lost."

But all of this seems to be missing the point and taking the movie far more solemnly than it asks to be taken. Basically, *9 to 5* is a light-hearted entertainment that shies away from getting truly serious about social issues, even though it does have a mildly feminist point of view. No one intended that the film would change the course of Western civilization.

Tomlin denies that *9 to 5* has a feminist "message." She says, "There's not really much you can tell people that they don't already know—it's not like we were trying to give them some big inside revelation or anything. The world's not so great for anybody in terms of the American dream and idea and everything. It's more like we're all in this thing together, dealing with life and living, and we tried to do something feeling and funny about it all. . . . What the film does is make you feel good about yourself, and if you feel good about yourself, you're not going to be treated like a second-class citizen." And, considering how enthusiastically audiences reacted to 9 to 5, it seems clear that the movie made a lot of people feel good.

Lily was pleased with the public's response to 9 to 5, which attracted a new audience for her who were not all that familiar with her past career. She remembers that the movie was a big hit even with her ninety-year-old Uncle Wallace, a farmer from Kentucky who drove all the way into town on two different nights to watch it. "When I first came on 'Laugh-In,'" Lily explains, "the show wasn't even particularly to my style, but I got an enormous amount of pleasure knowing that so many people were sitting down on Monday night to enjoy it. That movie, 9 to 5, was my first real hit, and I got the same feeling from it."

Just two months after the release of 9 to 5, Tomlin fans had a chance to see her again in *The Incredible Shrinking Woman*, an interesting 1981 film that may remind viewers of some of the clever sketches from her TV specials. The premise of this movie fantasy, directed by Joel Schumacher, is that housewife Pat Kramer (Tomlin) uses some household products that cause her, for reasons unknown, to begin shrinking down to the size of a child's doll. She becomes so small, eventually, that she lives in constant fear of being accidentally crushed to death by her husband, Vance (portrayed by Charles Grodin).

The Incredible Shrinking Woman delivers a hefty dose of satire aimed at the way that advertising and mass market techniques have come to dominate our lives. The film is full of tacky products, bright colors, and silly advertising slogans. In the bland California suburb of Tasty Meadows, where the Kramers and their children live, the biggest fear of all is . . . ring around the collar. Says Lily, "The movie is a valid response to a world in which corporate superpowers get bigger and bigger while the consumer feels progressively smaller and more helpless."

Once again Tomlin worked with Jane Wagner, who wrote the script for The Incredible Shrinking Woman. (And considering that their most recent collaboration, Moment by Moment, had been such a fiasco, Tomlin's decision to work with Wagner so soon again was a real tribute to her faith in Wagner's abilities.) Although Tomlin did contribute some of her own ideas to the story, she says that Wagner deserved to have the sole on-screen writing credit for the film. "I'm not a hardcore writer," Tomlin explains. "I can write things for myself—I've written pieces in the past . . . but I couldn't sit down and write a whole script. What I can do is contribute to a script or character, or pitch ideas. I like to be involved, and I always have been when I've worked in television. But movies are a different thing. I don't have that kind of experience, and I certainly don't have that kind of track record."

John Landis, who had been the director of National Lampoon's Animal House, was originally slated to direct The Incredible Shrinking Woman. He had hoped to do the film on a considerably larger budget, with some major technical innovations. One scene was to show a tiny Lily Tomlin delivering a speech on the steps of the Capitol in Washington. But the bigwigs at Universal, which produced the film, were none too pleased with his grandiose schemes, and he was later replaced by Joel Schumacher, who had written the screenplays for *Car Wash, The Wiz,* and *Sparkle.* "It was Joel's idea," Lily explains, "to make the whole thing look like Necco wafers."

Yet even in this scaled-down version, *The Incredible Shrinking Woman* presented a number of unusual problems for the filmmakers. There was no getting around the fact that the picture would have to show Tomlin's character progressively shrinking down to miniscule dimensions relative to the sets and to the other actors and actresses. Verna Fields, the executive in charge of the production for Universal, remembers, "After experimenting with Magicam and other optical processes to achieve the 'shrinking' effect—and spending considerable time and money—a decision was made to use oversized props. The live-action shooting of the film went well over schedule because of problems connected with building the oversized sets. A number of differently scaled oversized sets had to be created to give the illusion that Tomlin is continually shrinking. For example, a five-foot stretch of kitchen counter had to be built, eventually, into a mammoth sixty-foot-long set to create the illusion of a greatly diminished Tomlin."

Fields explains that many scenes had to be shot twice. When the Tomlin character appears on "The Mike Douglas Show," for instance, Douglas first filmed his part of the sequence by talking to an empty chair while being careful to look at the spot where the head of an eighteen-inch-tall person would be. Later,

Tomlin was photographed sitting in a gigantic prop chair, with footage of Douglas projected behind her.

Of course, giant props are nothing new for Lily Tomlin: fans will recall that Edith Ann is usually shown in an enormous rocking chair. "For years on my specials, I always went for big props," Lily says. "I had a big wallet and a big bacon, lettuce, and tomato sandwich. It was fun. It probably has to do with feeling culturally overwhelmed. In society the output, the hype is so massive and we are so infinitesimal in the long run—negligible, really."

The Incredible Shrinking Woman was based, very loosely, on a novel by Richard Matheson, which had been made into a movie entitled The Incredible Shrinking Man (1957). The earlier movie was a cautionary fable about the possible disastrous effects of radiation from atomic tests. The Tomlin version was a comedy not a horror film (at least, she hoped it would be), but it did retain the basic theme of paranoia concerning the unforeseen side-effects of modern technology.

In The Incredible Shrinking Woman, Pat Kramer is married to an advertising executive and is an enthusiastic user of any product that can be wrapped in plastic or sprayed from an aerosol can. Thus she unwittingly becomes a kind of guinea pig in a unique experiment. She begins to notice some unusual things. One is that her fingernails appear to be getting shorter. Then her bracelet drops into a bowl of breakfast cereal. And when she says good-bye to her husband one morning, he kisses her forehead. "Vance, our lips use to meet," says Pat.

The doctors are at first mystified by her strange

condition, but they figure out that she is shrinking due to a combination of the ingredients she has been exposed to in her perfume, hair spray, detergents, deodorant, nail polish, and numerous other products that she, as an avid consumer, has around her home. Yet when it comes to suggesting a cure for her affliction, the doctors can do nothing other than throw up their hands.

As Pat's height diminishes, her celebrity increases, and soon she is being interviewed regularly on network TV shows. At the same time, the country's largest corporations are determined that the cause of her predicament not be publicly revealed, for fear that it would make consumers less willing to buy their products. One company's officers decide to kidnap Pat; they plan to make a serum from her blood that, if introduced into the water supply, would shrink the whole world's population and leave these corporate executives as the giant rulers of the globe.

The Incredible Shrinking Woman includes several very funny scenes. One is when Pat makes her appearance on "The Mike Douglas Show." Jane Wagner's script takes aim at the kind of inane conversations that usually take place on TV talk shows, as Douglas asks vacuous questions and Pat responds in the smarmy manner of a newly anointed celebrity. She keeps flashing her toothy smile while Douglas pretends to be deeply concerned about her plight:

MIKE DOUGLAS: Has it all been a nightmare, Pat? Or has anything good come from this extraordinary experience?

PAT KRAMER: Well, Mike, I'll tell you. It has mostly been a nightmare. But some good things have happened, like getting to come on your show here.

One of the best features of The Incredible Shrinking Woman is the way the filmmakers created a unique look for Tasty Meadows. The first fifteen minutes are filled with quick shots of a Brave New World of pastel colors, overbright California sunshine, and apparently infinite amounts of consumer goods. The whole suburb, both indoors and outdoors, is like the lobby of a brand-new Holiday Inn, and everyone in it seems to live in a never-ending commercial.

The screenplay also has some nice touches that reinforce what the film is saying visually. In this pastel paradise, the life of the people is centered almost exclusively on buying products and keeping everything squeaky clean. (Of course, this is the perfect spot for somebody like Mrs. Beasley, whom Tomlin portrays in a number of scenes as a friend of the Kramers who loves to give out household hints to anyone who'll listen.) In Tasty Meadows, there are regular meetings of the residents of each block, and the chief topic of conversation is neatness; the neighbors accuse one another of not being as clean and tidy as possible. At another point in the movie we see Pat putting her children to bed. They request their favorite lullaby, and she sings it for them. What is odd—and amusing—about this is that the song, "I Wish I Was a Little Bar of Soap," is about a product.

Some other memorable moments in the film occur when Pat has shrunk to such a diminutive size that ordinary household objects have apparently become Brobdingnagian, and a threat to her safety. On one surreal occasion, a robot toy shoves her into a closet filled with battery-powered dolls and other toys. Pat rolls helplessly among these children's playthings, which, moving automatically, have become menacing monsters to her.

Tomlin's performance in *The Incredible Shrinking Woman* was a departure from anything we had seen from her previously. Lily's Pat Kramer is distinguished above all by her wonderful pluckiness. No matter how hopeless the situation, Pat tries valiantly to keep going ahead. She's always able to look on the bright side, even if she is about to be plunged inescapably into total darkness. Although she is less than a foot tall near the end of the picture, she still tries not to fall behind in her household chores. Cooking meals and washing dishes is not an easy task when you have to climb up to reach the stove, but Pat remains undaunted to the last. She's the epitome of the sweet and happy housewife. So sweet and happy is she (especially in view of her circumstance), that she seems a little crazy, too.

For all its strong points, however, *The Incredible Shrinking Woman* runs out of inventiveness before reaching its conclusion. The sinister plot to kidnap Pat becomes so silly and predictable that viewers may feel they've accidentally switched channels to a Saturday morning cartoon show rather than a Lily Tomlin film. In many ways the concept might have worked better as a sketch on one of Tomlin's TV specials. But as a full-length feature, the problem of devising a complicated plot and a rousing finale proved to be too much for the writer and the director. And that's too bad, for The Incredible Shrinking Woman has a number of excellent qualities that lift it above the level of the average movie comedy.

Once again the critics liked Tomlin's performance much more than they liked the movie as a whole. In Newsweek, David Ansen said, "Because Lily Tomlin is one of the funniest people alive, The Incredible Shrinking Woman provides a fair share of yucks. Also playing the consumer advocate Judith Beasley, Tomlin puts on a satiric display both touching and scalding."

According to Vincent Canby, writing in The New York Times, "Lily Tomlin's The Incredible Shrinking Woman is not the greatest comedy ever made, but it's most appealing and quite often hilarious. It's reassuring to see this immensely talented woman back doing the sorts of things she does best, after striking out gamely but completely in Moment by Moment. It's also reassuring to see the lines in front of the theaters playing The Incredible Shrinking Woman. Class still counts somewhere."

"Lily Tomlin shows a new, wistful charm," said Pauline Kael in The New Yorker. "Pat is probably the closest thing to an ingenue that Lily Tomlin has ever played, and she's more spontaneous in this role than she has been on the screen before. . . . It's a surprisingly free performance. You feel that Lily Tomlin is inside the character."

Some critics suggested that Tomlin was playing it too safe with this film. Richard Corliss's review in *Time* argues, "The movie is sometimes very funny. It also represents a waltz step toward popular acceptance by a performer tired of being worshiped by the few. Like former cult favorites Chevy Chase and Steve Martin, Tomlin has made a laff-a-minute movie that will offend nobody—except the comic's most ardent fans, who will buy tickets and then yell, 'Sell-out!'"

This point of view is in some ways understandable, but it's definitely unfair to Lily. The satire in *The Incredible Shrinking Woman* was in the same vein as that of Tomlin's TV specials from a few years before. The main difference between them is that the times had changed: what had once seemed daring now seemed fairly routine. In the early seventies it took a lot of courage to satirize some of America's sacred cows—or at least to do so on television, which was a much more conservative medium than the movies or the theater.

By the eighties the situation had changed considerably. In a way, Tomlin had been too successful at breaking down barriers. People such as herself and Richard Pryor, and programs such as "Saturday Night Live" and "SCTV," had tackled many previously taboo subjects during the seventies and early eighties. As a result, Tomlin's early routines are just as funny today, but they will seem much less risqué or venturesome than they did when first shown. It's hardly fair to blame her for failing to offend as many people in the eighties as she was able to offend in the seventies.

The *Incredible Shrinking Woman* was given a respectable, though unspectacular, reception at the box office. But *All of Me* (1984), Tomlin's next movie, was another commercial hit, winding up among the top money-makers of the year.

In *All of Me,* directed by Carl Reiner, Lily portrays Edwina Cutwater, one of the richest (and nastiest) women in the world. Steve Martin portrays Roger Cobb, a lawyer who, after a bizarre series of events, ends up sharing his body with the spirit of Edwina. She controls the right side of Roger, while he is in control of only his left half. The plot may sound complicated beyond any understanding, but the result of all these strange goings-on was one of the best comedies of the eighties. The movie features a number of wonderfully funny sequences, such as one in which Roger attempts to make love to an attractive young woman while Edwina does her best to sabotage his efforts.

Curiously enough, Tomlin was not all that enthusiastic about the project when she first saw the script. "When I first received and read the script, I didn't think there was any way that I could do it," she explains. "There was just too much stuff that was questionable. And I'm not the kind of person who goes around telling other creative people about their project. But I was encouraged to go and speak with Carl [Reiner] and Phil Robinson [the screenwriter]. So I said okay.

"What I liked about Carl and Phil was that they were pretty straight ahead and open, willing to discuss almost anything. If they had a real strong point of view they had it, and if they didn't they were real open. There was never any real investment in being right . . . if it was about something they didn't think was essential. I was impressed with that."

Tomlin remembers that what appealed to her about *All of Me* was "the idea of the male and female in the [one] body, and I thought it had a lot of potential for . . . the intimacy of it. And the kind of unconditional acceptance of one another . . . because you're sharing a physical body. It was the ultimate in intimacy."

After a few more rewrites of the screenplay, she was finally convinced "it could be a very funny, sweet movie. I didn't know how well it would turn out, but I thought it had a good chance. When we committed to do it and were all in it together to finish it and see it through, I knew it was going to be funny. I knew Steve was going to be really good in the physical comedy."

According to Carl Reiner, he had to do quite a lot of wooing to convince Tomlin to take the part. "It took a long time to get her in," he says. "She is very careful about what she does."

The basic idea for *All of Me* came originally from an unpublished novel, entitled *Me Two*, by Edwin Davis. Phil Robinson says he had to throw out most of what was in the novel when he wrote his screenplay. Robinson explains: "The book focused on the woman, who was very old, while the man whose body her spirit went into had almost no story. He was a bum off the street she'd never met before. The young woman the spirit was intended for was an unwilling participant, and the main thrust of the plot was how this man tries to keep her relatives from changing her will. All I liked [about the book] was the idea of a woman's soul entering a man's body. . . . And I thought it would be more sympathetic if the woman was denied a good first shot at life, so I made her bedridden.''

Once Tomlin had made a firm decision to appear in the film, she threw herself into the work with her usual intensity. She had long conversations with Steve Martin, Carl Reiner, and Phil Robinson before filming began, and they say she made several important contributions that went beyond her own performance. Martin explains that Tomlin was especially helpful when it came to getting his half-female, half-male act together. He was particularly grateful for small, feminine mannerisms—such as the way she rests her cheek on one finger—that she gave Edwina during her early scenes in the movie. "That way, when she came back inside me, I could use the same gestures," he says. And she showed Martin how she thought Edwina would walk. At first, he imitated Tomlin's walk with his whole body; later, he relegated the walk to his right side.

Robinson credits her with some other comic inventions, such as that of an elegant tissue dispenser of embroidered lace handkerchiefs, which she tosses away, like Kleenex, after each sniffle.

When filming was underway, Tomlin made a point of coming to the set every day, regardless of whether or not she was scheduled to perform. "There are scenes where we hear only her voice," Martin explains, "and those are usually recorded later. But she wanted to be there to feed me her lines, to make sure the timing was right.''

As far as her own work on the picture was concerned, she says, "I thought I had some good moments and I know that I made a contribution to the movie ultimately, which I'm happy that I did. . . . I liked myself in it. I didn't *love* myself in it. I thought I did okay." (Coming from someone as self-critical as Tomlin, this is high praise indeed.)

At the beginning of *All of Me,* we're introduced to Roger Cobb, who is trying to decide, on his thirty-eighth birthday, whether he should put all his energies into the law or into becoming a better jazz guitarist. He's highly dissatisfied with the uninspiring cases to which his legal firm has been assigning him (he tells a secretary, "I've been paying my dues for eleven years—I should own the entire club by now"), but he is also aware that his chances of striking it rich as a musician are very slim indeed. So he decides to give up jazz and buckle down to his legal work.

His firm then assigns him to settle the estate of Edwina Cutwater, a wealthy Beverly Hills spinster who has only a few days to live. Roger finds her to be as ill-tempered as she is rich and eccentric. Edwina barks "Gas me" to her servants when she needs oxygen, and she treats Roger like an errand boy. She matter-of-factly informs him of her scheme to die and then come back to life in the beautiful, healthy body of a young woman, Terry Hoskins, who is the daughter of her stable man. What's more, Edwina intends to inherit her own wealth in this strange transmigration scheme. Roger attempts to inject a note of rationality into the proceedings, but is rebuffed:

EDWINA: Guess what I'm going to do? I'm going to come back from the dead.

ROGER: Oh? And what makes you think you can do that?

EDWINA: Because I'm rich.

Unfortunately for Edwina (and fortunately for *All of Me*), when the moment of her death occurs, her soul is sent into the body not of Terry Hoskins but of Roger Cobb. Most of the film is concerned with the comic predicament of Roger and Edwina sharing the same body. They both try to get her soul into the body of Terry, who, we soon find out, is after Edwina's millions. At first, Roger and Edwina are repelled at the thought of living at such close quarters, but eventually they come to care about each other.

A typical amusing scene from the movie occurs when Edwina endeavors to cool Roger's lust while he tries to satisfy his physical desires for Terry. He is sitting up in bed as lovely blond Terry unbuttons his shirt and caresses him. Meanwhile, Edwina is thinking of "very old nuns . . . and dead kittens."

Lily found Edwina to be an especially interesting character to play. "She can be prudish, arrogant, haughty, and infuriating," explains Lily, "but beneath it all she has dimension, she's real." She was able to sympathize in many ways with the lonely heiress. "Edwina was born with incredible wealth and an incurable heart. At one point she recalls her childhood, when her nurse would wheel her oxygen tent to the window so that she could watch other children play in her gardens and ride her horses. . . . All that Edwina wants out of another life is the first one she never had."

Edwina, as Tomlin so adeptly portrays her, has much more substance than the typical crazy rich ladies we see in many movie comedies. Tomlin gets her best chance to show us Edwina's personality in the scene in which she tells Roger some of her biggest regrets about her life. Lily makes the most of this poignant moment; it's a finely tuned bit of acting—well understood, carefully planned, and executed with touching understatement. Says Edwina: "Mr. Cobb, I've spent a lifetime shackled by frailty and poor health . . . I've had all the money in the world and not one good chance to enjoy it. I have never been to Europe. I've never been anywhere, really. Sure, I've *ordered* from Neiman's and Gucci's, but I've never actually been there. I've never ridden my horses. I've never been to the ballet, never danced." (In many ways, Edwina seems like a character that Tomlin might have invented for her one-woman shows.)

Edwina disappears into Roger's body, but by no means does Tomlin disappear from *All of Me*. We hear her voice whenever Roger hears Edwina's thoughts. Furthermore, whenever Roger looks into a mirror, he sees Edwina's reflection rather than his own. Carl Reiner explains: "It's a logical device, given the premise, and it enables the characters to have moments together which would otherwise have been monologues. . . . We could hardly have asked Lily Tomlin to give one of her best performances almost entirely off-screen." Careful viewers of *All of Me* will note the nifty timing involved in several of the sequences that show Martin and Tomlin reacting to each other through a variety of different mirrors.

The chemistry between Lily Tomlin and Steve Martin contributes a great deal to the film. They're both uninhibited physical comedians: unlike most performers today, they would have had the ability to have been great comedians in the silent movie era, too. Curiously, their best scene together in *All of Me* occurs during the final credits, and may have been missed by those moviegoers eager to get to the exit quickly. In a mirror, we see Roger and Edwina exuberantly dancing together. What's wonderful is the total lack of restraint they both show during this goofy dance of joy. It's not only the happiest moment of Edwina Cutwater's life, but it wouldn't be surprising to learn that it might have been Lily Tomlin's happiest moment as well.

Steve Martin is given many opportunities to show off his flair for physical comedy, and he responds with a bravura performance. His walk is irresistibly amusing, an ingenious bit of androgyny. His left leg moves forward with a masculine stride; his right leg minces in an extremely feminine style. Martin says that the hardest part of learning the walk was figuring out how to do the masculine half. He explains, "There's something to do on the woman's side; the man is just you. You have to ask yourself what's normal."

Martin's most complex acting challenge, however, was in the courtroom scene. Viewers will recall that Roger is then about to try a vitally important case— but he falls asleep at this critical moment, leaving Edwina temporarily in sole possession of his conscious mind. She must "take over" for him, even though she knows next to nothing about the law. Here we see Martin acting as he believes Edwina would imagine Roger would act. And, astonishingly, Martin is able to convey all of this to the audience. He was pleased with the way the scene turned out: "One of my fears was making the transitions between Roger and Edwina clear and crisp enough. And there is a moment in that courtroom, when Roger's body pushes back in his chair but Edwina is in control, that you definitely have the feeling someone else is there."

The reviewers were almost monotonous in their praise of *All of Me*, especially regarding the performances of the two stars. For instance, Janet Maslin wrote in *The New York Times*, "Some things simply have to be seen to be believed, and the sensational teamwork of Steve Martin and Lily Tomlin in *All of Me* is one of them. If this, the best American comedy since *Tootsie*, doesn't have you in stitches, check your vital signs: you may be in as much trouble as Edwina Cutwater. . . . It's Mr. Martin and Miss Tomlin, doing his and her best work in films thus far, who are at the heart of the film's success, especially when they abandon their animosity and generate the warmth to become friends."

In *Commonweal*, Tom O'Brien said, "*All of Me*, in short, is a sassy, endearing tour-de-force. It is frequently compared with *Tootsie*, but in truth Steve Martin outdoes Dustin Hoffman: he has to be both male and female without benefit of costume changes. Tomlin comes across far more powerfully than *Tootsie*'s pallid women." Susan Sworkin, writing for *Ms.*, commented, "Steve Martin gives an amazing performance. And Lily Tomlin is perfect playing her natural extremes—mega-whacky and mega-heartbreaking."

But the excellence of *All of Me* is based on more than just the acting of the two leading performers. Credit must also be given to the fine screenplay, which is reminiscent of some of the classic screwball comedies of the thirties, such as *Bringing Up Baby*, *Nothing Sacred*, and *My Man Godfrey*. The eccentric rich people, madcap events, swift pace, and inspired slapstick of *All of Me* are in the same vein as the humor of those unforgettable movies. The basic situation of *All of Me* is also familiar to fans of thirties' comedies: two people who at first loathe each other are brought together, and in the end come to appreciate each other's finer points.

The supporting cast features several amusing performances, such as Richard Libertini's as a blissed-out guru named Prahka Lasa. The guru speaks no English—he merely repeats a few of the words that people say to him—yet he manages to get more than his share of laughs. His eyes almost seem to be shining with light from some otherworldly source. Also worthy of mention is Madolyn Smith, who plays Roger Cobb's fiancée, Peggy. When she gets infuriated with Roger in one scene, she tells him off by yelling, "I think jazz is stupid . . . And I faked all those orgasms." Then she proceeds to make some ecstatic noises, only to conclude by saying, "Sound familiar?" Roger then replies, feebly, "Yeah, well I faked mine, too."

As a director, Carl Reiner works well with actors,

but he doesn't have much of a sense of how to tell a story visually. Many of the jokes in *All of Me* aren't really thought out cinematically: we have the sense that he merely uses the camera to record the performances of the cast. After all, Reiner's formative experience was primarily in television, and he has never totally broken away from his old habits. Still, this is a little more than a quibble as far as *All of Me* is concerned. The lively humor of the script and the inventive performances of the cast make *All of Me* Tomlin's all-around best film.

During this period when she was rehabilitating her reputation with movie critics and audiences, Tomlin also continued to appear from time to time in television comedy specials. *Lily: Sold Out*, for example, was one of her finest. Shown February 2, 1981, on CBS, this special depicted a visit by Tomlin and her various impersonations to Las Vegas.

At the beginning, viewers see Tomlin finishing a performance of *The Seven Ages of Woman*, a Broadway revue that bears a more than passing resemblance to *Appearing Nitely*. She is soon offered an irresistible sum to take her one-woman show to Caesar's Palace in Las Vegas. At first Lily is determined not to compromise the integrity of her show, which clearly has a feminist point of view, but in the end she sells out with a vengeance (hence the title *Lily: Sold Out*) and does her act in the glitzy Vegas tradition of shameless excess. Lily descends onto the stage of Caesar's Palace in a giant egg, as neon lights flash all around her. At one point she is shot out of a cannon and during another routine she makes an entrance while riding a motorcycle.

Besides seeing Ernestine, Mrs. Beasley, and Tess, the shopping bag lady (who harasses guests at the hotel entrance by shouting, "Permit me to allow you to enter!"), viewers were also treated to one of the few male characters ever done by Tomlin, in this case a guy she named Tommy Velour. Tommy is without a doubt one of Tomlin's most inspired creations. He's a Vegas crooner whose every movement is excruciatingly artificial. He has slicked-back, oily hair and a weasely mustache, and he wears outfits that seem to be made of nothing but sequins.

Tomlin's impersonation of him is so perfect, in fact, that it's almost eerie. If we saw Tommy's number out of the context of a Lily Tomlin special, it would be difficult to be sure that he was being played by a woman. Tomlin certainly has every move of her portrayal down pat, from the way she holds a cigarette to the frenetic way she snaps her fingers. Her sly grin and slightly raised eyebrows are terrific, and her singing style makes use of nearly every show-biz-cliché mannerism, familiar to anyone who has seen the acts that perform in Las Vegas.

Tommy's big moment in the special is his production of a song entitled "If I Ruled the World." He sings, "People ask me what I would do if I ruled the world/Every dude would have a chick to behold/All the records would turn solid gold." At one point Tommy seems to be perspiring heavily, so he undoes a few buttons on his shirt, revealing an (apparently) hairy chest beneath.

Lily describes Tommy as "the penultimate lounge act ... a composite of Wayne Newton and Robert Goulet and Steve Lawrence and Sammy Davis." She says, "I worked hard on Tommy Velour. I tried to mount his Vegas act for the first time in a small San Francisco club called The Boarding House. I didn't tell my audience it was in the context of my special. I just said it was a new piece."

The response of this audience, she remembers, was less than favorable to her first attempt at playing Tommy Velour. "I got a lot of letters telling me it was a huge mistake. Lousy. No content. I felt kind of empty."

But this negative reaction only made her more determined to get every detail of the portrayal just right. After a few more weeks of hard work, she finally succeeded, to her own satisfaction, in capturing the essence of the character. "Tommy's bravado is so magnificent that it's uplifting," she explains. "Tommy's just perfect; he's a hero."

Besides Tomlin's usual entourage of characters, *Lily: Sold Out* includes some brief guest appearances by Paul Anka, Liberace, Audrey Meadows, Joan Rivers, Dolly Parton, and others. The best of these is Jane Fonda's performance as a bag lady who hangs out with Tess.

One of the most interesting aspects of this special is the way that Tomlin frequently makes fun of herself. Of course, she parodies the Las Vegas entertainment scene mercilessly—yet she is almost as hard on Lily Tomlin. Several of the funniest barbs are aimed at her own record as an actress with a social conscience nearly as heavy as the Rock of Gibraltar. For instance, when Lily's agent first tells her about the Vegas gig, she says it would be demeaning for her to accept the offer. She says to him, "I don't think I could live with myself if I did something just for the money." But her opinion changes quickly when she hears more of the details. "*How* much? . . . Is that per *week*? . . . Next stop, Caesar's Palace!" And when rehearsals begin for the show, Lily at first resists her agent's demands for more pizzazz and less politics, yet winds up giving a performance almost as flamboyant as Tommy Velour's.

Television critics had mostly good things to write about *Lily: Sold Out.* In *The New York Times,* John J. O'Connor commented, "The combination of Lily Tomlin and television still works beautifully. . . . Miss Tomlin's creations inevitably operate on several levels. She is having fun with them while at the same time liking them intensely." Tom Shales, writing for the *Washington Post,* said, "There's something delicate, immaculate, and sweet about *Sold Out,* even when it's at its most outrageous. . . . There's only one Lily, and it isn't enough."

On the other hand, James Wolcott offered this sharply dissenting point of view in the *Village Voice:* "Unlike Carol Burnett, Tomlin isn't able to satirize show-biz flamboyance from the inside; she keeps herself at a snide distance, signaling to her fans that she's smarter than the showboats she's mimicking. . . . I found myself wishing that Tomlin's gallery of eccentrics could be stuffed like puppets into a trash-bin and carted off. . . . Tomlin fussed over her characters' quirks as if they were expressions of ragged good-ness—of an inner grace uncontaminated with contact with the straight world. Compared to the static and complacent hysteria of *Sold Out*, the sane world seems like heaven."

The Emmy Award voters didn't share Wolcott's opinion, fortunately for Tomlin, and named *Lily: Sold Out* the "Best comedy, variety, or music special" of the 1980–81 TV season. It was Tomlin's fifth Emmy. Of course, the credit for the high quality of the show goes not only to Lily (who was one of the executive producers), but also to Bill Davis, the director, and a team of writers, headed up by Jane Wagner (who was the other executive producer).

A little more than a year after *Lily: Sold Out*, Tomlin was back on CBS in another special, *Lily for President?*, which was broadcast May 20, 1982. This show was concerned with a fictional plunge by Tomlin into politics. Lily runs for President on the "Stop It" platform. "Anything you want stopped," she says, "Lily will stop it for you—hunger, inflation, pestilence."

As might be expected, Mrs. Beasley, Edith Ann, Ernestine, and Tess join Lily's political bandwagon, but the most significant aspect of the special was the introduction of three new characters to the Tomlin gallery—Holly Oneness, Agnus Angst, and Purvis Hawkins. They are all singers who appear at a fund-raiser that successfully fills the coffers of Lily's campaign. Holly Oneness is a sixties-style protest singer. Agnus Angst is a punk rocker, a member of a New Wave group called the Manic Depressives. (She will later play an important role in *The Search for Signs of Intelligent Life in the Universe.*) Agnus sings about all the things that make her angry, and the list is a long one: cable TV, Pac-Man, crime, Detroit, Hollywood, and the older generation are just a few of the subjects that provoke her wrath. Purvis Hawkins is a black male soul singer, complete with a neatly trimmed beard and mustache. "The best word I can think of to describe Purvis is luscious," Lily says. "Purvis is expansive, elevated, easy, real smooth in a wholesome way." *Lily for President?* also featured cameo appearances by Howard Duff, Sally Field, Jane Fonda, and James Garner.

The reviewer for the *New York Daily News* suggested that viewers "just sit back and spend an hour with Tomlin and her crowd of old friends and watch how one of our most creative comic minds weaves her magical web of humor."

Tony Schwartz, writing for the *Times*, said, "Miss Tomlin retains a remarkable ability to bring her characters alive by balancing a deft sense of parody with a genuine affection for them. . . . [Her] constantly growing family of characters continues to give her the distinctive identity that her movie roles have not."

Tomlin explains that programs like these have given her a special kind of satisfaction: "Television lets me have a chance to play around with different fantasies. I love to see my characters dressed up. When we were shooting the special [*Lily for President?*], there were doubles for all of the characters, and it seemed perfectly natural to see them walking about the set. To me, they're real people."

Lily thoroughly enjoyed her work on TV and in the movies during this period, though she admits she was also yearning to get back on the stage. Occasionally in the early eighties she performed *Appearing Nitely* for short runs at various theaters around the country. Still, she says the scheduling of the movies "prevented me from a lot of other activities, not intentionally. I very much wanted to go out and tour a little more."

"I love to go to a new town and settle in," she told a reporter in a 1982 interview. "I've done the show [*Appearing Nitely*] for three or four weeks at a time in places like Houston, Denver, Chicago, and Minneapolis. It's a way to get to know a city, make friends—and the show runs a lot better and a lot smoother than it would if you just did one-nighters."

Lily gave unmistakable evidence of her intense devotion to the theater with her decision not to do any other movies immediately after the popular success of *All of Me*. In 1984, with several recent hit movies to her credit, Tomlin could very easily have gone on to appear in more films—and be paid quite handsomely for her efforts. She was in the enviable position at that time of being flooded with offers for other parts. Instead, she decided to return to the theater in her most ambitious project so far.

Tomlin appears with Tom Smothers and David Steinberg on "The Music Scene," a short-lived variety series on ABC. (PHOTOFEST)

On "Laugh-In," Tomlin, as Mrs. Earbore, exchanges pleasantries with Rita Hayworth. (PHOTOFEST)

Without a doubt, the most popular of Lily's characters is Ernestine, the telephone operator. (PHOTOFEST)

Lily as Edith Ann on The Second Annual Comedy Awards. (PHOTOFEST)

Linnea (Tomlin) sings in a gospel choir in a scene from *Nashville.*
(PHOTOFEST)

Lily sings along with a Muppet on a Lily Tomlin special.
(PHOTOFEST)

Ira Wells (Art Carney) and Margo (Tomlin) solve a difficult case together in *The Late Show*. (PHOTOFEST)

One of the most intimate sequences between Tomlin and Travolta in *Moment By Moment* is in a Jacuzzi. (PHOTOFEST)

The characters played by Dolly Parton, Lily Tomlin, and Jane Fonda are all dissatisfied with their jobs in *9 to 5.* (PHOTOFEST)

In *The Incredible Shrinking Woman,* Pat Kramer (Tomlin) becomes so small that children's toys become menacing monsters. (PHOTOFEST)

Mrs. Beasley gives out some household hints in *The Incredible Shrinking Woman*. (PHOTOFEST)

Lily takes a fictional plunge into politics in her 1982 CBS Special, *Lily For President?* (PHOTOFEST)

Steve Martin and Lily Tomlin dance exuberantly at the end of *All of Me.* (PHOTOFEST)

Lily Tomlin and Bette Midler each play one of the two sets of identical twins in *Big Business.* **(PHO-TOFEST)**

CHAPTER 10

SIGNS OF INTELLIGENT LIFE ON BROADWAY

The story of how Tomlin's latest Broadway hit, *The Search for Signs of Intelligent Life in the Universe*, came to be written and developed is an interesting drama in itself. For over a year she tried out different bits of material at various spots around the country, including performances in Atlanta, Austin, Boston, Denver, San Diego, Sante Fe, and Seattle. She put on scores of these "work shows," with Wagner continually rewriting the play. Sometimes Tomlin would be reading material onstage that Wagner had written only hours before. "We'd hand out these leaflets," Tomlin explains, "announcing an evening of 'Genuine Fan Torture.' Our company manager would get us these great deals in motels for twenty dollars. We were desperate for small places to play in so the press wouldn't find us. In Los Angeles we rented a storefront, built a little stage nine-inches high, hung lights and blankets, and brought people in from the streets to see the show free." She says she was able to keep expenses down by traveling with a minimal entourage—just herself, Wagner, a company manager, a stage manager, and someone to handle the lights and sound. (Needless to say, Lily doesn't have to worry about the demands of a supporting cast of performers, since she is able to fill all the roles herself.)

Throughout this period, Wagner was producing "reams and reams" of material, according to Tomlin. "Jane has no compunction about giving me twenty or thirty pages of single-spaced material that's scratched through and penciled over and that might take me three or four days to retype."

Says Wagner, "I write long, and something that begins as a fifteen-minute monologue becomes three or four minutes in the show."

Their collaboration is not always harmonious; they often get into some fairly heated arguments over what lines should be dropped from a script. "But we are forgiving of each other," Wagner says. "There's always a give-and-take, and there's a chemistry that comes from this that makes you both reexamine where you are. In arguing, the input creates another perspective from the one either of you started with."

Tomlin explains that the reactions (or lack thereof) of the audiences at the work shows have a considerable influence on the tailoring of the material for a play. Sometimes it can be almost maddeningly difficult, she admits, to figure out why something may not be working: "I wonder if it's just me, or maybe the lines, or maybe the crowd on this particular day." What she is aiming for is that "the whole thing pull together and become something complete. . . . And then, yeah, you start tinkering. I'm skilled in knowing that the juxtaposing of something totally alters other things, too. And I might choose the wrong place to put it. But if I believe in something I would go a pretty long time before I would abandon it. And I wouldn't necessarily abandon it because it didn't get a laugh, unless that was really the purpose of it."

But Tomlin adds that all of this reworking and tinkering can be highly satisfying: "It's something that fascinates me. . . . There are so many aspects of it, like creating a transition from one piece to another might suddenly give a whole other direction to it. . . . It's like inventing something—there's no formula for the process."

With *The Search for Signs*, Tomlin was determined that Wagner share fully in the public attention that the play received. For one thing, Tomlin insisted that her name appear on the marquee of the theater in letters nearly as large as her own. "In the past, I was given all the credit and the glory," Tomlin says. "I didn't think there should be any question about how this project evolved."

During the inevitable standing ovations that followed performances of *The Search for Signs*, Tomlin would typically say to the audience, "I thank you. I thank you. I thank Jane Wagner!" Wagner even came out onstage after the opening-night performance to take her bows next to Tomlin. "Through her generosity of spirit, Lily orchestrated it so I'd get attention that I didn't even want—but that's good for my career," says Wagner. "On opening night, when they were giving me that kind of wonderful acceptance, it was an incredible psychological victory. You can't even say it was a dream come true, because I didn't even have a dream like that."

Wagner explains that the triumph of *The Search for Signs* was especially sweet for her because it followed by only a few years the disaster of *Moment by Moment.* "After *Moment,*" she says, "Lily could have never wanted to work with me again, but she did. That was really courageous." (To this comment Tomlin responds, "It wasn't courageous from my point of view. Nobody could write for me like Jane could.")

From the beginning, Tomlin and Wagner intended that *The Search for Signs of Intelligent Life in the Universe* be a major step forward for them artistically. Whereas *Appearing Nitely* was closer to the free-form, surrealistic structures of TV sketches and stand-up routines, *The Search for Signs* was much more of a real play. The characters cross each other's paths in the storyline of *The Search for Signs,* and many of the jokes are thematically related to each other.

As Tomlin says, "This show is more complex, more intricate, deeper than anything I've done before. There is a connection in this show that didn't exist in *Appearing Nitely.* That was good, but this is much better. It has more of everything. It's on a higher verbal level, it's more inventive, it's funnier. . . . Jane had a real vision for this show. I feel like we've really created something wonderful."

Some of the Tomlin characters in *The Search for Signs* were new ones, and they tended to be a bit less eccentric than some of the older characters, such as Ernestine and Edith Ann. (Tomlin's portrayal of Lyn in the play is the outstanding example of this trend.) Apparently, Tomlin was at first reluctant to move in this direction, and Wagner says she had to be talked out of relying too heavily on the more familiar characters. "She always felt safer doing characters that she knew, that were somehow connected to her childhood," Wagner explains. "I told her that to grow, she had to try out new characters."

For that reason, *The Search for Signs* was "a much more demanding show to master," according to Tomlin. "Because they were less outrageous, it took longer for me to find the fluidity to wheel between the characters."

At the beginning Tomlin was concerned that becoming too realistic would take the edge off her humor. But Wagner was determined to find a way of being funny yet at the same time being more true to life. Wagner explains, "For a while now people have been using black humor to be mean-spirited. It's so easy to be shrewd and mean. I thought we needed something else. We needed something loving." She feels that *The Search for Signs* reflects a feminine sensibility in its style of humor. Says Wagner, "I wanted to move away from macho humor, which is attacking and aggressive. I wanted us to laugh at ourselves and love ourselves. There's a compassion and tenderness to the humor. Ironically, it's more daring today to be tender."

The Search for Signs was a big risk for Tomlin and Wagner—in more ways than one. Financially, they took the chance of suffering a huge loss, since they were the sole investors in the show (Tomlin signed all the payroll checks). But more than money was at stake. In a show of this kind there is a staff— publicists, stage hands, lighting technicians, and sound mixers—but finally it all comes down to Tomlin and Wagner alone. Wagner writes the words and Tomlin performs them; each is dependent on the other, and on virtually no one else. Furthermore, because of their earlier success with *Appearing Nitely*, the expectations of the press and the theatergoing public would be much higher than before.

When *T.S.F.S.O.I.L.I.T.U.* premiered on Broadway September 26, 1985, at the Plymouth Theater, it was immediately obvious that Tomlin and Wagner had created one of the most popular plays of the season. Tomlin says she was pleased that audiences "were laughing so hard, it added ten or fifteen minutes to the show. . . . And people also started writing us and telling us that they were touched by the humanity in the show. We got a kind of serious mail that we never got before."

The critics were nearly unanimous in calling *The Search for Signs of Intelligent Life in the Universe* the biggest triumph of Tomlin's career. The show received some of the most euphoric notices of any new play produced in the eighties. In *The New Yorker*, Brendan Gill (who's known to be hard to please) wrote, "From start to finish, Tomlin's energy never flags; it is we in the audience who are brought figuratively to our knees, and by our applause at the final curtain express . . . our admiration for Tomlin's art." And Frank Rich, a drama critic for *The New York Times,* said, "As the star trails like a comet through a galaxy of characters—with no props, costume changes, or scenery for artificial propulsion—so Miss Tomlin attempts to sum up a generation of social history in a tightly compressed saga of a few representative lives."

The Search for Signs was praised in such glowing terms that it's difficult to imagine how Tomlin, when she next decides to do another one-woman show, could ever top the reception she received for this play. "Tomlin is the best thing that has happened to Broadway in years," said the critic for *Women's Wear Daily.* *Newsweek*'s reviewer called the show "a human comedy that strikes home so sharply it brings gasps of recognition as well as outbursts of laughter." Clive Barnes, writing for the *New York Post,* commented, "I could almost wish that I had not praised [*Appearing Nitely*] so much, so I could have saved even more praise for this. Because *this* really is in a different league."

The Search for Signs of Intelligent Life in the Universe eventually won Tomlin the Tony Award in 1986 for "Best Actress in a Play." It was a well-deserved honor, especially since the play was the best vehicle to date for showing off Tomlin's wide range of acting abilities. In it Tomlin gets to do over a dozen of her best characterizations. More so than with any of her previous endeavors, we are dazzled by her facility in this show for remaking herself into whomever she is supposed to be at that moment. She manages these changes so fast that she reminds us of the way the Road Runner cartoon character is in a certain place one instant—and the next, somewhere else. We can't imagine how Tomlin goes so quickly from one character to another without any hint of a transition.

The main narrator in the show is Trudy, the shopping bag lady. She is the one who, with some help from her extraterrestrial "space chums," is conducting the search mentioned in the title of the play. But several other characters are just as important—such as Agnus Angst, the fifteen-year-old punk rocker, and Kate, the bored socialite. The most intriguing characters of all of those in the play are Lyn, Edie, and Marge: they are three feminists whom we see going through most of the important social and political changes of the seventies and eighties.

The Search for Signs is a good example of how Tomlin's (and Wagner's) brand of humor differs from that of most comedians. The usual way that most comedy works is by ridiculing characters who pretend to be better than the rest of us. We naturally laugh when we see our presumed "betters" depicted as actually no better than anybody else. Thus, the targets of most comedians are those who occupy positions of status or who are held in esteem by many people. Most jokes are aimed at politicians, celebrities, lawyers, doctors, business executives, ministers, and others of higher than average status in the world. Tomlin's comedy, on the other hand, works in the opposite way: she reveals what we have in common with people who are assumed to be less significant or important than average. Tomlin shows us the humanity of those in whom it might not at first be apparent, such as Trudy, the shopping bag lady, and Brandy and Tina, two prostitutes who have important roles in *The Search for Signs*. In a Tomlin routine, we are usually laughing *with* the characters rather than *at* them.

Another key point about *The Search for Signs* is that it clearly has a feminist perspective on the world. And yet the play doesn't at all seem to be a piece of propaganda, with an obvious social or political message to deliver. Instead, Tomlin and Wagner are just as tough on those who share their opinions, such as Lyn, Edie, and Marge, as they are on those who don't.

In an article for *Ms.*, Marilyn French wrote, "*The Search for Signs of Intelligent Life in the Universe* is the first work I know of that simply takes it as a given that a mass audience will accept feminist attitudes, that proceeds on the assumption these attitudes are shared and that therefore does not lecture, hector, or even underline." Interestingly, French says that when she once remarked to Wagner that the show was a breakthrough, and couldn't have been put on Broadway ten years before, "Jane Wagner looked at me with surprise: 'You think so? I don't know. I guess we're so involved with what we're doing that we don't think about how it will be received. Not that it doesn't matter to us . . . but maybe we aren't really on that wavelength.'"

Frank Rich also took note of Tomlin and Wagner's feminist outlook. In his review for the *Times*, he called *The Search for Signs* "the most genuinely subversive comedy to be produced on Broadway in years. It's a radical critique not only of the national status quo but also of some activists who have fought for change."

What makes *The Search for Signs* an entertaining play (and what Broadway audiences responded to) is not so much the feminist viewpoint, however, as the delicious characterizations in the show. Trudy is certainly one of the best of these, and she is given a more important role here than in any of Tomlin's other projects. (Trudy is for all intents and purposes the same character as Tess from *Appearing Nitely*. Wagner and Tomlin chose to use a different name in this show because Trudy was formerly "a designer and creative consultant for big companies," while Tess's background was supposed to be quite different.) At the beginning of the play Trudy tells us that she wears an umbrella hat through which she has been communicating with a group of aliens from a distant galaxy. "My umbrella hat works like a satellite dish . . . I pick up signals that seem to transmit snatches of people's lives . . . It's like somebody's using my brain to dial-switch through humanity."

From Trudy we find out that her space chums are puzzled by our obsession with physical fitness and distressed that we have no "metaphysical fitness program." From their alien perspective, "Earth is a planet still in its puberty. In fact, from their planet, earth looks like it has pimples." Trudy tries, though not always successfully, to explain humanity to these aliens. And, together, Trudy and her space chums try to make a scientific study of the human race.

Tomlin clearly has fun playing Trudy, with her raspy voice and stooping walk, yet she still makes us believe there's a real person underneath all the eccentricities. In Trudy's first scene, for instance, we see the hostility she feels toward all the "normal" people who believe themselves to be superior to her. On a street corner she yells to passersby, "You look away from me, tryin' not to catch my eye, but you didn't turn fast enough, did you?"

Trudy says, "Since I put reality on a back burner, my days are jam-packed and fun-filled. Like some days, I go hang out around Seventh Avenue; I love to do this old joke—I wait for some music-loving tourist from one of the hotels on Central Park to go up and ask someone, 'How do I get to Carnegie Hall?' Then I run up and yell, 'Practice!' The expression on people's faces is priceless."

One of the characters that Trudy and her extraterrestrial friends observe is Chrissy, portrayed by Tomlin with much enthusiasm and a sensational amount of energy. Chrissy is a plucky young woman who spends most of her time at health clubs and self-improvement seminars. She's engaged in a never-ending search for good-looking men and for a better sense of self-esteem—though unfortunately she seems to find little of either. Chrissy keeps trying to stay thin, but she admits that "I have gained and lost the same ten pounds so many times over and over again, my cellulite must have déjà vu."

It's touching (and very true to life) to listen to Chrissy expressing some of the anxieties that many of us feel. She is unhappy that she hasn't been able to find a job that's right for her, no matter how many different positions she tries. "I'd do better at something creative," she says, "but somehow I lack talent to go with it, and being creative without talent is a bit like being a perfectionist and not being able to do anything right." What's more, Chrissy explains, "It's not that I lack ambition. I am ambitious in the sense that I want to be more than I am now. But if I were truly ambitious, I think I'd already be more than I am now."

Kate is another of Tomlin's best characterizations from *The Search for Signs*. She's a jaded socialite who has become bored with just about every aspect of her life. Kate is tired of her lover, and intends to split up with him soon, because "It's one thing to tolerate a boring marriage, but a boring affair does not make sense." She is so wealthy that she is able to spend most of her time having her hair done and reading magazine articles about the latest trends. She is concerned that "having everything can sometimes make you stop wanting anything." Some of Tomlin's expressions, while she's doing Kate, are truly priceless. Kate looks down her nose so often that Lily's face appears to be even longer than usual. Another good touch is how Lily uses her hands when she's playing the character. From her delicate movements, we can tell that these are fingers that have never come into contact with garbage bags or dishwashing detergent.

Agnus Angst, the teenage punk rocker, wears so many chains and zippers that garage doors flap open when she passes by. She is furious with the world in general and, above all, with her father in particular, a biologist who kicked her out of the house after she spit into a petri dish in his laboratory. She angrily says, "He's working on some new bio-form he thinks he'll be able to patent. He doesn't get it that I am a new bio-form."

Agnus winds up staying with her grandparents, Lud and Marie (both played by Tomlin), who don't know what to make of her strange behavior. They're real down-home, small-town types: Marie, Agnus's grandmother, is usually sewing, while Lud, her husband, puffs away on one cigarette after another and squints through the clouds of smoke around his head. They quarrel endlessly, like many old couples, but without ever really getting nasty with each other. This is a typical exchange between Lud and Marie:

LUD: You know what your problem is, Marie? Too negative. You're too negative about ninety-two percent of the time.

MARIE: Yes, and about ninety-two percent of the time I am dead right.

LUD: Oh, hell, if you're so damn right all the time, how come we have . . . a pink-haired punk granddaughter [with] the manners of a terrorist?

The Search for Signs includes many outstanding scenes and notable characterizations, but the centerpiece of the play is the section that takes us through over a decade of the women's movement as seen and experienced by Lyn, Edie, and Marge. The most important of the three is Lyn, whom we first see at an E.R.A. rally and who by the end of the play is trying to make sense of those years "when we actually thought we were changing the system—and all the time . . . the system was changing us." She eventually comes to the realization that, "It's hard to be politically conscious and upwardly mobile at the same time."

When Lyn first meets Bob, her future husband, she feels she has found the perfect mate for a feminist. "He was the only man I've ever known who knew where he was when Sylvia Plath died," Lyn remembers. And when they met, Bob was wearing a T-shirt that said WHALES SAVE US. Later, Lyn starts to worry that he may be becoming a little more sensitive than is good for him. "Maybe Bob has gotten too much in touch with his feminine side," she says at one point. "Last night, I'm pretty sure, he faked an orgasm."

But when their children are born, Lyn soon realizes how difficult it is to be a career woman and a housewife at the same time. Her anxieties are compounded by the fact that she has twins, and "hyperactive" ones, to boot. Lyn says, "When they turned three, my doctor prescribed Ritalin—I wouldn't dream of giving drugs to my children, but it does help when I take it myself." Lyn can barely keep up with her boys' demands, because "At some point, they looked at one another, and realized there were two of them and only one of me."

Lyn and Bob's marriage finally reaches its nadir when she discovers that he has been having an affair. "All those nights you were gone . . . I should've known you couldn't have that many aikido classes each week," she tells him. Following this incident there's a touching scene at a doctor's office where Lyn expresses some of her frustrations: "You're sure, doctor?" she asks. "Premenstrual syndrome? I mean, I'm getting divorced. My mother's getting divorced. I'm raising twin boys. I have a lot of job pressure—I've got to find one. The E.R.A. didn't pass, not long ago I lost

a very dear friend, and . . . and my husband is involved . . . not just involved, but in love, I'm afraid
. . . with this woman who's quite a bit younger than I
am . . . And you think it's my period and not my
life?"

Lyn's story captures a feeling of the sadness of
many lives similar to hers. She has a confused sense
of despair and loss, and even though Lyn is very intelligent she is not especially adept when it comes to solving her own problems. Tomlin and Wagner have
definitely succeeded in taking someone out of the real
world and bringing her to life on the stage.

Despite all the excellent observations throughout
the play, it gets a little pretentious at times, especially
near the end when Trudy comes out and muses on the
Meaning of Life and what she calls the "goose bump
experience." Wagner's text yearns to be something
more than amusing, more than just a lot of witty lines
and nicely realized characters. For example, in one
scene Trudy tells us: "On the way to the play, we
stopped to look at the stars. And as usual, I felt in
awe. And then I felt even deeper in awe at this capac-
ity we have to be in awe about something." When
Trudy says this, we in the audience may feel that it
would have been better if she had kept quiet for once
rather than waxing eloquent. We may also feel that
Trudy isn't necessarily more profound than the rest of
us, she just has better writers.

Wagner says that much of her inspiration for writing the play came from her reading of books such as
The Tao of Physics. "What I started with was the
quantum inseparability principle," she explains. "I

had started to read science, and to realize that phys-
icists today are saying what metaphysicists said two
thousand years ago. We're all connected; we all time-
share the same atoms and the same time here on earth.
I wanted to show those connections." Unfortunately,
Wagner's ideas about science and philosophy don't
necessarily have a lot to do with most of the characters and situations in the play. When she writes about
people, Wagner has the sympathetic imagination of a
fine novelist, but when she philosophizes, she often
sounds more like a college sophomore breathlessly
talking about her first class on Plato.

Tomlin fans may have a few qualms about some
of the lines in the text, but nearly all of those who saw
her performance have nothing but praise for the star of
The Search for Signs. Above all, one can't help being
astonished by the energy and enthusiasm she puts
into her work. She is onstage for over two hours and
obviously goes all-out for every minute of that time.
The unflagging vigor of her performance reminds us
that she was once a cheerleader in high school, and
that she approaches her work with the zeal that most
people lose as adults. Even when she appeared on talk
shows to promote *The Search for Signs,* it was obvious that she was no typical show-biz celebrity doing
another plug, but instead was someone who genuinely
loved doing the play and would talk about it to anybody who wanted to listen.

When she makes her entrance at the beginning of
the show, Lily bounds out onstage in tuxedo pants
and a black, red, and violet-striped blouse. She bows
low, gives the audience a broad, toothy smile, and

quickly begins the play. Although she never changes costume, she's still able to leave no doubt as to which character is speaking at any given time. Like a good mime, she is able to make body language into an art form. She can stiffen her back and become Kate, and a few minutes later she may be leaping around the stage as Agnus Angst.

Lily says that before she goes onstage she is filled with nervous energy. "I'm moving around nonstop, saying 'Good evening' to everybody backstage, going over my lines out loud, pacing around, checking my body mike, finishing my hair, seeing if my clothes are in order. . . . Five minutes before the curtain goes up I'm saying, 'What time is it? Oh God I'm late, oh God I'm late.' It's kind of a mantra, I guess."

Two other people who made noteworthy contributions to the show are Otts Munderloh, the sound designer, and Neil Peter Jampolis, the lighting designer. At key moments in the play their inventive lighting and sound effects add some nice touches to underline what Tomlin is doing and saying. We see smoke bombs going off, strobe lights flashing, headlights turning on, and candlelight flickering. Meanwhile, we hear brakes screeching, packages rustling, doors slamming, and waterbeds gurgling. Members of the audience may not be all that aware of these effects while the play is in progress, but without them many of the jokes wouldn't work as effectively as they do.

After appearing on Broadway during the 1985–86 theatrical season, Tomlin took the play on tour, with extended runs in Los Angeles and San Francisco, throughout most of 1987. Late in 1986 *The Search for*

Signs was published as a book (the text was credited solely to Wagner), and it became the first play in over twenty years to appear on the national bestseller lists.

Yet another tribute to the popularity of *The Search for Signs* was that when the "Nova" science series on PBS put on a program in November 1986 about the possibility of intelligent life in space, they hired Tomlin to narrate and to play Trudy and Ernestine as well. When asked what would happen if alien beings tried to contact the earth and reached Ernestine at her switchboard, Lily says Ernestine would first tell them to "deposit another fifteen cents, please." And so, "The one chance we'd have to talk to them, she'd put them on hold! We'd lose them forever." Lily says she has tried to imagine Ernestine as a space traveler, but somehow the image of Ernestine traipsing across Mars in those platform shoes is a trifle bizarre, to say the least.

In the works are plans for a cable TV film and a record album of *The Search for Signs,* but until these materialize, Tomlin fans who didn't catch her performance in person can see her doing parts of the show in *Lily Tomlin,* a documentary film that was released in 1986. *Lily Tomlin* was directed by Joan Churchill and Nicholas Broomfield, who followed Lily and her entourage through many of the work shows for *The Search for Signs.* The idea was to capture a behind-the-scenes view of the creative process of putting a play together. The film, which also includes some interviews with Tomlin and a few clips from her TV specials, builds to the climax of opening night on Broadway.

This sounds as uncontroversial as could be imagined, yet *Lily Tomlin* ended up as the basis of a series of lawsuits. All went smoothly at first, according to Joan Churchill, but before the documentary could be released to the public, Tomlin filed a lawsuit to prevent its distribution. She asked for $6.25 million in damages, claiming that her privacy had been invaded and that so much of the play is shown in the film that her own ability to sell the show to cable television had been impaired. In response, Broomfield and Churchill filed a countersuit for $11 million.

The upshot of all these legal wranglings was that a Superior Court judge from Los Angeles ruled in August 1986 against Tomlin's bid for an injunction against the documentary. But the filmmakers didn't come out with an unalloyed triumph: they were forced to distribute *Lily Tomlin* themselves after professional distributors decided not to handle the film.

This brouhaha might lead viewers to expect a movie filled with scandalous revelations and embarrassing moments. But in spite of these anxious expectations, Tomlin fans can rest assured that if they watch the documentary, they will get through the entire film with their eyebrows firmly unraised. *Lily Tomlin* is a straightforward, professional record of the making of *The Search for Signs of Intelligent Life in the Universe*. We never really catch Lily off-guard in any kind of revealing moment: the closest we get is when we learn that she is capable of devouring a hot dog in four bites.

When Superior Court Judge Jack M. Newman denied Tomlin's injunction, he wrote in his decision,

"For the Court, viewing the film—twice—has only enhanced interest in seeing the show in its entirety. Parenthetically, for what it's worth, Ms. Tomlin, for whose creativity and talents the Court has great admiration, is most favorably presented in all aspects of the film, including the close-ups." (For what it's worth, the Court is a pretty good movie critic.)

The documentary certainly provides fans with a fascinating glimpse of a Tomlin work-in-progress. We get to see her in a much looser type of setting than we usually find her. The audiences at her work shows bear with her as she tells them, "This is a very embryonic show, and pieces of it are still rough." During many of the routines, Tomlin yells out sound cues and tries to explain what's missing from the then-current version of the script. She often talks to the audience about her intentions concerning the show, and she ad-libs when one of the jokes doesn't get a laugh. After one sketch, for example, she says, "By your response I see there aren't too many hard-core Mrs. Beasley fans here . . . I guess you decided that for $7.50 you'd just try me out, huh?" On occasion Lily will actually come right out and admit, "Sorry, I blew that line."

The documentary also provides us with several glimpses of Cheryl Swannack, Tomlin's hard-boiled road manager. This forceful woman is shown as being highly protective of Lily. In one sequence we see Swannack coercing some New York billboard artists into applying more paint to get just the right amount of twinkle in Tomlin's left eye on a gigantic advertisement for the show. Another person who makes a brief appearance in the movie is Peggy Feury, who was Tomlin's acting coach at the time she was putting together *The Search for Signs.*

Joan Churchill explains that she and Nicholas Broomfield "wanted to make a film about someone we really admired." Previously, Broomfield and Churchill had collaborated on five other documentaries, which were concerned with mental hospitals, prisons, and several other topics. They first approached Lily with the idea for the documentary in 1983, and it took a while to convince her to cooperate. In the end, though, Churchill says the final version of the contract "gave us total and complete creative control" over the editing of the film. The only exception was that Tomlin retained "kill rights" to all material shot in her home and her dressing rooms.

After months of seeing Lily at close range, the filmmakers were highly impressed by her acting skills and by her relentless drive in achieving her goal of a successful show. "I've never seen a person work harder in my life," Churchill says. "Lily's mind is like a computer. She was usually far ahead of the crew."

Despite all their differences in the courts, "I am still a fan of hers," says Churchill. "I do think she's the greatest comedian around. . . . The minute she'd get onstage, she'd just sort of exude something that was wonderful to watch.

"We showed the film to Lily when it was done and she was very complimentary," Churchill remembers. "She seemed surprised at how much of the process we were able to grasp. You see, she thought it was going to be some boring BBC-type documentary. It wasn't until later that the other shoe dropped."

Churchill feels that the people around Tomlin were more to blame for what happened than the star herself. "We're puzzled. It isn't Lily Tomlin here. It's a machine—agents and lawyers with dollar signs in their eyes." Churchill believes that the turning point in the whole affair came when Lily's managers and lawyers realized "the potential financial windfall from a hit Broadway show. You have to remember that when we first approached her, no one knew that what we would be filming would ultimately become one of the biggest hits of the Broadway season."

Still, there's no denying, in spite of Churchill's generous comments, that Lily was clearly in a position to overrule her advisers and withdraw (or, better yet, never file) her lawsuit. The argument that viewers of *Lily Tomlin* will be disinclined to watch her in a possible film of *The Search for Signs* is an extremely dubious one. Indeed, this way of thinking involves the same kind of paranoia that we often associate with Lily's characters, but not with Lily herself. As Trudy the bag lady says, "I refuse to be intimidated by reality anymore."

The one obvious shortcoming of the film is that it is, if anything, too restrained in giving us an intimate or personal look at Lily Tomlin. It's unmistakable throughout that she is very guarded whenever she's being photographed anywhere other than on the stage of a theater. Far from prying into her privacy, the documentary is actually very respectful of her at all times. Vincent Canby observed in his review of the film for

The New York Times that, "From start to finish, Miss Tomlin is seen as if photographed through a bullet-proof plastic bubble, designed to protect her from the movie-making terrorists."

We must keep in mind, however, that it's not necessarily anyone's fault that the picture turned out the way it did. Lily is essentially a private person, and she is not the type who enjoys baring her innermost soul to the cameras or to the gossip magazines. (After all, one has to wonder at the state of mind of those who actually enjoy discussing in public the intimate details of their personal lives.) And the filmmakers had no choice but to work with their subject on the terms she offered.

Churchill suggests that she is "extremely uncomfortable just being Lily Tomlin. . . . Lily would either play directly to the camera or ask us what we wanted from the scene. It took us far longer to accumulate any footage that didn't feel staged than we had imagined."

Furthermore, "I think Lily is terrified of letting people see how terrified she was, especially on opening night, and I think it's that vulnerability that makes her so lovable."

What the documentary reveals about Lily is that she is a woman who expresses herself best when she's playing the part of someone else. She has great confidence in her ability to take on the role of another person, but when it comes to those moments when she has no performing to do, she is as unsure of herself as the rest of us are.

CHAPTER 11

BIG BUSINESS

Lily has always been especially fond of projects that give her the chance to play more than one character, so her decision to appear in *Big Business* seemed perfectly natural. *Big Business*, which was released in 1988, is concerned with the comic predicaments of two sets of identical twins, born on the same day in the same hospital and accidentally mismatched at birth. Lily Tomlin and Bette Midler each play one of the two sets of identical twins.

The prospect of doing another multiple-character movie was what intrigued Tomlin. From the time she first read an early version of the script, she saw *Big Business* as a "vehicle where I could do something closer to what I do on stage and on TV, to fill the characters out with details and eccentricities." She even says she had "always wanted to do a twin movie. I'd gone to twin conventions in the past and made myself acquainted with twins. . . . There's something great about the sight of three or four hundred pairs of twins in one room. I wanted to do the kind of twins who if they were traveling and there was only one bar of soap, would have to cut it in two so they each could have a half. That would run to my taste—something really bizarre."

The basic situation in the movie—the mixing up of two sets of identical twins—is an idea with a very distinguished pedigree indeed. The best-known example of the genre is Shakespeare's *The Comedy of Errors*, but the Roman playwright Plautus covered some of the same ground over two thousand years ago in a comedy entitled *The Menaechmi*. Much more recently, the idea was used in *Start the Revolution Without Me*, a 1970 film starring Donald Sutherland and Gene Wilder.

Dori Pierson, who with her writing partner Marc Rubel created the screenplay for *Big Business*, admits frankly that the initial concept for the movie was patterned after *The Comedy of Errors*. She adds, "Marc and I also did research on identical twins separated at birth. We tried to make it as realistic as possible." When Pierson and Rubel started *Big Business*, they were trying to create a vehicle for Bette Midler and Dolly Parton.

The first time Midler read the screenplay, she was not particularly impressed. "The core was there—a farce about mismatched twins—but everything else was different," recalls Midler. "There was a much more venal set of characters. It was really overwritten and I couldn't make much sense of it." Midler then turned to Leslie Dixon, who had been responsible for *Outrageous Fortune*, to do a rewrite, which Midler says was "terrific"; later on, Tomlin brought in Jane Wagner for some more reworking of the script. Nevertheless, Pierson and Rubel were the sole writers to receive screenplay credit for *Big Business.*

The premise of the movie obviously presented a considerable number of problems for the director, Jim Abrahams. Would he use the traditional split-screen method of photographing a person twice in the same shot? Or was there a better way? At one point he experimented with some sophisticated rubber masks—cast from Tomlin's and Midler's faces—which were worn by doubles who had been hired because their facial bone structures matched those of the stars. But the masks made them "look like they were dead," according to Abrahams. "The masks were a complete bomb."

Abrahams remembers that many special effects experts he consulted with then recommended that he cast real twins instead of trying to find some way of solving the difficult technical problems. For obvious reasons, this answer wasn't satisfactory to Abrahams or to Disney, the production company financing *Big Business.* Next to the task of finding two sets of real identical twins, each with the box-office appeal and acting abilities of Midler and Tomlin, almost any other undertaking begins to seem insignificant.

What the director and producers came up with was a new process using a computerized camera system that had been tried only once before, on *Who Framed Roger Rabbit?* "There's always been a confined feeling to twin movies," explains Michael Peyser, one of the producers of *Big Business.* "In the

Patty Duke days, the two Patty Dukes had to be in the same plane, the same distance from the lens, and there had to be a split down the middle that was a straight line. What makes this movie different is that by using computers we can move and pan and dolly the camera and re-create the identical camera movements for both characters. The computer is like a missile-guidance system."

With the aid of a computer, the cameras on *Big Business* were able to reproduce their moves precisely, but for the actresses this way of shooting scenes presented quite a challenge. Tomlin and Midler had to remember what they had done in a particular shot, and then respond to their earlier performance as if it were happening in front of them. "You not only have to be accurate," explains Tomlin, "you have to be comedic and have some rhythm and play. . . . Sometimes you wonder if you're really performing at all. I mean, because you're so wrapped up in the physical business of being so precise about everything, standing on your mark and looking at the right spot at the right time."

To top it off, Tomlin and Midler had to learn to deal with each other, which turned out to be at least as great a challenge as the technical problems. The trouble was that while Tomlin is meticulous and detailed in her preparation, obsessed with getting everything perfect, Midler is loose and improvisational and appears not to take her work at all seriously.

Between takes, Tomlin would spend every available minute trying to find the right gestures for her characters. Sometimes she would talk to Jane Wagner about what to do in the next scene. And Tomlin hired an acting coach, Susan Batson, to help her find the right "eccentricities and details" for her characters in the movie. Batson would write comments on yellow Post-it notes after each take, and an assistant would deliver them to Tomlin.

Meanwhile, Midler would be found either playing with her daughter, Sophie, who was about one-year-old when the movie was shot, or reading. (Curiously enough, we might expect Tomlin to be the intellectual and Midler to be a very light reader, but in fact Midler is usually seen with a volume of Kierkegaard or Baudelaire or some other serious author.)

Tomlin admits she and Midler "really had a hard time meshing. We were so different." Midler agrees that, "We have two very different processes. I admire her process—I'm sure she doesn't admire mine. I'm so slovenly. She spends a lot of time thinking about gestures and props and bits that will make the character whole. I'm more spontaneous." Midler says that at first she felt bad that she hadn't done the kind of homework Tomlin had done. "But my way to find my character is different."

During the first few days on the set, the two actresses were perpetually getting on each other's nerves. But after hours of quarreling, with insults flying back and forth, Midler and Tomlin would become so exhausted they wound up doubling over and laughing so hard they cried.

"I got her laughing one day," remembers Tomlin. "I was so proud of myself, because she just had to sit down on the floor. We got onto this whole thing about the Midler Institute of Mugging. I'd be working *internally* and trying to evolve something, and she'd say, 'Come on—lighten up. Every scene can't be an Academy Award–winner.' And then she was getting into all this mugging—you know how she does it—with that big jaw, her eyes, everything. Those classic mugs. So I started practicing to see if I could mug as well as she could.''

Midler describes herself as "the founder and guiding light of the Institute of Mugging. . . . We give an introductory course in Basic Mugging. Then you can go on to Advanced Scene Stealing, Mugging with Body Parts, Mugging with Food, Mugging with Sticky Substances, and How to Destroy Your Director with Mugging. It's a rich curriculum." By the time *Big Business* was completed, both actresses say that they had become good friends and actually enjoyed making the movie so much they might do another together in the future.

Tomlin has complimentary things to say about Midler's accomplishments as an actress: "Very few people have done in a leading role what Bette has done in [her] comedies. . . . She's played characters that are not particularly likable in the conventional sense—they're ballsy, strong, and pushy—and yet Bette makes them totally appealing. Bette has broken through something. All the guy comics play characters who do despicable, greedy, aggressive things, and women don't usually get to play those parts."

What happens on-screen in *Big Business* involves even more complications than those that took place on the set. At the beginning of the picture two sets of twins are born on the same day in a hospital in Jupiter Hollow, a small Appalachian town. One pair of twins is born of parents from Jupiter Hollow; the other of wealthy parents from New York, who just happen to be passing through that part of the country at the time. A nurse accidentally mixes the babies up, so that one from each family winds up in the wrong crib. No one notices the mistake. The rich girls are named Rose and Sadie Shelton. The poor girls are named Rose and Sadie Ratliff. (Bette Midler plays both Sadies, while Lily Tomlin plays the two Roses.) When the girls grow up, we see that they don't know about the mix-up; nevertheless, they have remained true to the characters of their natural parents. The Roses are country girls at heart who love nature and honest people. The Sadies, on the other hand, love the bright lights and comforts of the big city. Inevitably, the Bette Midler character from Jupiter Hollow dreams of escaping to New York, and the Tomlin character from New York seems out of place in her job as a business executive.

All goes well until the Moramax corporation, run by Rose and Sadie Shelton, makes a decision that threatens to have a disastrous effect on Jupiter Hollow. The country Rose and Sadie decide to raise a fuss, and they head for New York to protest the actions of Moramax. All four of them take rooms at the Plaza Hotel, and soon even the most alert viewer may have trouble recognizing which character is which as the complications multiply. In the climax of the movie, patterned after the mirror scene from *Duck Soup*, each of the characters finally learns of the existence of her identical twin. With mutual shocks of recognition they at first freeze, then begin screaming until all four are nearly hysterical. At the end, Jupiter Hollow is saved from devastation by the country girls and Rose Shelton. Midler's Sadie Shelton turns out to be the only one with no sympathy for the plight of the residents of the small town.

The more appealing of Tomlin's two characters is Rose Shelton. Because we've seen how discontented she is with her life in New York, it makes the audience feel good when we see her fall in love with a straightforward, nature-loving man from the country (played by Fred Ward). Never one to settle for the easiest laughs, Tomlin tried to make her characterizations as complex as the screenplay would allow. "The rich Sadie, played by Bette, is very pulled together, very confident," Tomlin explains. "So I played my character, the rich Rose, very scattered. Bette is very materialistic, and I am much more spiritual—I come in with a stray dog, with paw prints all over my clothes, and my shoulder pads are constantly slipping . . . I don't fit in the corporate world at all. I love nature; I go to the park all the time."

In order to bring the right qualities to her performance as Rose Shelton, Lily deliberately made herself short of breath before the filming of a scene. She would roam around the set, mumbling her lines, rolling her eyes, making weird little animal noises, and—just before the camera rolled—turn a few pirouettes. (This is obviously not a technique a less-famous actress could easily get away with.) Says Lily, "I do it to make myself dizzy and vague—like Rose."

The rich Rose from New York may be a bit scatterbrained, but the poor Rose from Jupiter Hollow is "strong, confident, and assertive," according to Lily. "She has more fundamental, wholesome values. I tried to make the two characters different so they would be clear on the screen. There is so much information for the audience because of the mistaken-identity plot, you had to be sure the audience knew who was doing what at what time so they could be in on the joke."

Tomlin succeeds in her attempt at differentiating the characters as much as possible. The rich Rose is a touchingly droll person, while the poor Rose has some of the same flinty qualities as, for instance, the Sally Field character in *Norma Rae*. Rose Ratliff may also remind us of some of the characters from Tomlin's comedy routines. Marie, in *The Search for Signs*, is another no-nonsense woman who's from a small town and is suspicious of big-city ways.

Reviewers treated Tomlin kindly for her work in *Big Business*, although they weren't always quite as flattering in their comments as they had been in the past. Richard Corliss said in *Time* that, "Tomlin is an adept dear, and has a fine time hexing Moramax's corporate wimps with her voodoo snake whammy. Still, you may vainly search for signs of the quicksilver wit and emotional risk she radiates onstage. Someday Hollywood will harness her genius, in some movie with a different co-star. After all, who looks at anyone else when Bette Midler is around?"

In spite of her apparently casual approach to acting, Midler's performance in *Big Business* is just as effective as Tomlin's. Both Roses have some nobler impulses, but the Sadie characters are pure lust and appetite, regardless of whether the objects of their desires are sex, food, money, clothes, or power. In *The New Yorker*, Pauline Kael pointed out that, "Sadie Ratliff is the most recognizably human of the comic creations—a supplicant abasing herself before the world's goodies. She watches *Dynasty* over and over, and dreams of being Alexis; her eyes dance when she looks in Cartier's windows."

Sadie Ratliff yearns for luxuries as intensely as a condemned prisoner yearns for freedom. When she and Rose Ratliff get a first look at the sheer opulence of their rooms at the Plaza, Sadie is enraptured by every detail. Upon entering the bathroom she says, "Cute little soaps in the shape of swans! Could you die!"

It's a delight to watch Midler in action. Her comic walks are a highlight of the movie: she moves her ample, top-heavy body around on perilously high heels. When one of her characters is pleased with herself about something, she can strut with such abandon that she virtually radiates a sense of ecstasy with each step.

Most of the time *Big Business* manages to provide viewers with breezy entertainment. Yet on the whole the movie is not one of Tomlin's best. What's good about *Big Business* is, almost exclusively, the performances of the two stars. Apart from them there really isn't much else, except a farce that creaks along like an old piece of rusty machinery.

From the moment we know that the four characters are converging on the Plaza, we can already predict most of the jokes that are coming. We know there will be some near-misses at the elevators, some mix-ups with confused hotel desk clerks, and so forth. Too much of the humor is based on the gimmicky premise of mistaken identities.

Another irritating feature of the movie is that most of the residents of Jupiter Hollow are cornball stereotypes of rural people. Viewers may get the impression that the screenwriters' and the director's closest acquaintance with small-town America is through watching episodes of old sitcoms such as "Green Acres" and "Petticoat Junction." From the point of view of most Hollywood movies, it seems that virtually all of the U.S., outside of parts of New York and California, is one vast Hickville in which all the men wear suspenders and smoke corncob pipes, and all the women wear red polka-dot dresses and yodel a lot.

Abrahams's direction of *Big Business* is fairly pedestrian, and the movie has the look of being the latest product of the Disney Studio factory rather than the product of particular individuals. The cause of the trouble was apparently the age-old one of too many cooks. Of course, making Hollywood movies is always a collaborative effort, but *Big Business* involved even more collaboration than usual.

Says Abrahams: "I think it was my job in terms of directing Bette and Lily just to sync up the movie with their talents. Far be it from me to tell them how to be funny. When they suggest something, I should have my Directors Guild card burned if I say no." What this meant in practice was that scenes would have to be shot in a number of different ways in order to accommodate everyone's preferences. One take of a scene might be as Midler wanted it, another take the way Tomlin wanted it, another as Abrahams had originally planned it, yet another might combine elements of several of the previous takes, and so on. Any undertaking as involved as that of shooting a film is best done with one strong person firmly in charge, at least most of the time.

Big Business was one of the most popular movies of the summer of 1988, though it didn't turn out to be quite the blockbuster that Disney executives had hoped for. Most of the critics tended to have positive things to say about the movie. Richard Corliss wrote in *Time*, "It's value for money to get two fish-out-of-water stories in one, especially with the planet's two most gifted performing females in the main roles." In *The New Yorker* Pauline Kael said, "The picture moves along, spattering the air with throwaway gags, and a minute after something misfires you're laughing out loud." David Denby, the reviewer for *New York*, called the movie as a whole "dumb," yet admitted "This is not the fault of the actresses, who are both wonderful in each of their two parts."

For her next movie, Tomlin is planning to star in a comic remake of *The Three Faces of Eve*, which was originally made in 1957 with Joanne Woodward in the leading role. The script for the new version is being written by Paul Rudnick, and the story is concerned with the problems of a woman with multiple personalities. (Will Tomlin ever again be satisfied to play just one role in any project?) Another possibility is for Lily to reprise her performance as Linnea in a sequel to *Nashville*, which would once again be directed by Robert Altman. "This time Linnea will be running for governor of Tennessee," says Tomlin. "At least those are the plans Altman has so far." The sequel has been tentatively entitled *Nashville, Nashville*. Tomlin and Midler have also discussed the chances of their reuniting in another movie, but considering how choosy Tomlin is in selecting scripts, fans probably shouldn't be breathlessly expecting to see them together again any time soon.

While she waits for shooting to begin on *The Three Faces of Eve*, Tomlin will be performing *The Search for Signs* in a few more cities. But much of her time is taken up reading scripts for projects she's considering. She says she is getting a substantial number of film offers these days, and she attributes this mostly to the success of her play.

But Lily firmly intends not to be rushed into anything. "I find it hard to accept a movie role, period. It's so collaborative, and if you're very far apart in your sensibilities, it's really tough to reconcile all those opposing points of view." Lily plainly expresses her attitude on the subject when she sighs and says, as she has on more than one occasion, "Comedy is so hard."

CHAPTER 12

A REAL PERFECTIONIST

Those who have seen Lily Tomlin at work all agree that she is a real perfectionist. She pushes herself harder than anyone else ever could. And she positively insists that those who work with her do their jobs as well as they can be done. In fact, there are times when she expects other people to do more than they may be able to do.

On a stage or a movie set Lily is a dynamo of energy, but she also possesses great discipline to go along with her vigor. She immerses herself totally in a character and prepares everything beforehand. She is able to be brilliant on take after take before the camera, in spite of any difficult conditions on the set. Sometimes her co-workers say that she seems to feel that she is just warming up, even after ten or fifteen takes of a scene. "She works harder than anyone I've seen in my life," says Robert Benton, who directed her in *The Late Show.*

Just about everybody else who knows Lily concurs with Benton's description. Says Jane Fonda, "Yes, Lily's a perfectionist. She creates something new with each take. It's fascinating to watch her developing her character, and she's never completely satisfied even though she's quite wonderful in the movie."

Lily has been this zealous in her pursuit of excellence since her early days in the coffeehouses and cabarets. "When I was starting out," she remembers, "I made friends sit in my kitchen and listen to the same monologue at least a hundred times. They didn't want to hear it, but I needed to know if the damn character was right. You work it, work it, and work it. Then, when you're onstage you try it, and they either laugh, cry, or sit there slack-jawed for an interminable length of time." Without a doubt, Lily believes in the value of hard work as intensely as any Bible-thumping preacher believes in the value of following the Ten Commandments.

She prefers acting on a stage to acting in the movies, "because in the theater there are an infinite number of opportunities for me to perfect what I'm doing. Movies are fun, and I always try to do my best . . . but the theater is special for me." Most actors say they begin to tire of a role after they have been performing it regularly for a long time, yet Lily says she enjoys doing *The Search for Signs* every bit as much today as she did when she first began working on it five years ago. Furthermore, "I like the theater because it doesn't involve all the collaboration that you get into with a movie."

When Lily does agree to appear in a film, "I'm not

just some actress who goes to work and doesn't care how it comes out or what they do with me. I'm just as concerned with what they do with the other actors, ultimately. If I'm going to be in a project and I'm going to be identified with it, then I want to know that it's putting out something that I want to be identified with. It's just caring about the project. I'm going to fight about something if I don't like it and I think it should be different."

Of course, not everyone is thrilled by the prospect of working with somebody who's obsessed by a search for perfection. Lily's steely determination, and her sometimes thorny temperament, make her not necessarily the easiest person to deal with in a professional situation. On occasion she has been known to chew out film crews who aren't doing their best. And she isn't afraid of taking on directors and co-stars.

Bette Midler says, "Sometimes everybody else, including the director, would be satisfied, yet she would still want to do another take. . . . She might suggest that I use a particular gesture—and I would usually resist the idea at first. But in the end I would often decide that she was right and use her suggestion after all."

As an example of the sort of thing that went on frequently during the making of *Big Business*, Midler recalls how Tomlin asked her to develop more "stage business." In one of the sequences in which Rose Shelton's shoulder pads keep sliding out of place, Tomlin urged Midler to push them back, "like a big sister cleaning me up." Midler says, "I told her I didn't want to mess with that." But after Tomlin repeatedly persisted with her advice, Midler finally gave in and followed her suggestion.

Jim Abrahams, the director of *Big Business*, says that Tomlin was aware of a great many details about the characters that no one else on the set had even begun to think about. "Lily knows literally whether the character brushes her top teeth before her bottom teeth," explains Abrahams.

Part of what drives Lily's perfectionism, it seems, is her fear that she may inadvertently make a mistake of some kind that would humiliate her before an audience. She admits that she spends a lot of time "worrying about what I would do if something of mine that I'm not proud of turned up in the public eye." Lily's life is obviously one that is filled with more than her share of anxieties, yet it's largely because she worries so much that she is able to excel so consistently as a performer.

Not surprisingly, then, producers and directors say that getting her to agree to appear in a movie is no easy task. "She was definitely a hard sell," remembers Carl Reiner, her director for *All of Me*. "Lily will only commit to a project if she is satisfied that she is going to be in nourishing hands."

Lily is the first to agree. "I only want to do something if it's really good. . . . I never just *take* a part." The list of movie roles she has turned down is a long one, and she says she has no regrets about those chances she missed. "Even if it happened that something I turned down became a huge hit, it wouldn't bother me that much because I just couldn't make myself do something if I wasn't absolutely convinced at the time that it was worthwhile. Otherwise, what's the point of it all?"

Comedy, to Lily, is a very serious business. She doesn't believe that work of high quality is done by those who adopt a casual attitude toward what they're doing. "Even when I'm being funny, I'm deadly serious," she comments.

Lily derives a great deal of satisfaction from her work, especially when it is going well for her. "Acting is like therapy for me," she says. "A word or a gesture may uncover facets of my life I may not have been aware of. Sometimes it doesn't—but either way, it certainly cuts down on my shrink bills."

Lily has always been a private person who is most at ease with people she has known for a long time; she's never been all that comfortable in social situations. She has a strong antipathy for gossip columnists and those familiar tabloids that are sold at supermarket checkout lines. "I have never been able to come to grips with the public's need to know everything," she says. "I love acting, but I also cherish my privacy."

One side effect of the single-mindedness behind her dedication to acting is that, like many other workaholics, Lily has few interests outside her profession. She doesn't really have any hobbies, doesn't travel much (apart from touring with her one-woman shows), and rarely goes to concerts or movies. She does, however, have one strong interest which has never ceased to fascinate her: people watching. Everywhere she goes she studies people compulsively. Lily is absorbed by the differences she finds between people. She appreciates unique gestures and eccentricities; in fact, she relishes these nuances with the delight of a connoisseur.

Says Lily, "I'll be driving the car and see someone with a great look or walk, and I'll go around the block just to observe them again."

Sometimes she'll tape the conversations of people she meets. Lily recalls an occasion when she tried to get close enough to tape the conversation of two bag women in Los Angeles: "It's rare to see two of them together, and these two were like girlfriends. But when I tried to get near, pretending I was waiting for somebody, they would clam up or move away."

Many of Lily's co-workers have had extremely flattering things to say about the quality of her acting. Richard Pryor has called Tomlin "a goddamn national treasure. I'd drop anything, anywhere, to work with her." Robert Altman, her director in *Nashville*, says she's "a genius." According to Robert Benton, the director of *The Late Show*, Tomlin is "the greatest living American actress. She transcends comedy."

All of this praise, whether from directors or actors or critics or fans, tends to make Lily a bit uncomfortable when she hears it. She says she has learned to be wary of most forms of success and acclaim. "If your work is satisfying and success is a byproduct, that's a nice gift," she explains. "But when it's just a part of the hype . . . that's different."

"I'm not looking to get any more famous," says Lily. And she jokes that "Sometimes I worry about becoming a success in a mediocre world."

Lily says her twenty-five years of experience in

show business have taught her that the feeling of being successful is relative: "When I would go to the Improvisation and I would wait until three o'clock in the morning to do five minutes and there would be four couples left, if one person would come up to me and say, 'You're great! Where did you get that stuff?'—it would be just like being on the cover of Time."

I N D E X

ABC, 38, 60, 68, 69
Abrahams, Jim, 179, 187, 188, 194
Academy Award nomination, 77, 80, 93
Alda, Alan, 68
All of Me, 3, 136–145
Altman, Robert, 77, 78, 79, 80–81, 82, 84, 87
And That's the Truth, 64–65
Appearing Nitely, 3, 61, 93–105, 151, 156, 158, 162
Ashley-Famous, 36
Aykroyd, Dan, 75

Batson, Susan, 181
Beatty, Ned, 81
Below the Belt, 37
Benton, Robert, 87, 191, 192, 196
Big Business, 177–188, 193, 194
Blakley, Ronee, 78, 83
Boarding House, The, 94, 147
Broomfield, Nicholas, 38, 170, 171, 173

Café Au Go-Go, 29
Carne, Judy, 49, 59
Carney, Art, 87, 89

Carradine, Keith, 81, 82
Carson, Johnny, 63
Cavett, Dick, 85
CBS, 60, 65, 67, 68, 145, 149
Churchill, Joan, 38, 170, 171, 173–174, 175
Coleman, Dabney, 122, 124–125
commercials, 36
"Cracked Belle" award, 46
Crenna, Richard, 65

Davis, Bill, 149
"Dick Cavett Show, The," 71–72
Disney Studio, 179, 187, 188
Dixon, Leslie, 179
Draper, Ruth, 28–29
Dreyfuss, Richard, 68

Emmy Award(s), 3, 61, 67–68, 69, 75, 86, 93, 149
nominations, 65
Everett, Chad, 71–72

Feury, Peggy, 173
Fields, Verna, 116, 129
Fonda, Jane, 119–120, 121, 122, 126, 147, 192

Garfunkel, Art, 86
"Garry Moore Show, The,"
35–36, 41
Gibson, Henry, 48, 59, 78, 82, 83
Gilbert, Bruce, 120
gold record, 57
Grammy Award(s), 57, 93
nominations, 61
Grodin, Charles, 86, 127

Hawn, Goldie, 48, 49, 50, 59
Higgins, Colin, 119, 122, 125

Ice House, The, 57–58, 94
Improvisation, 29, 30, 32, 197
Incredible Shrinking Woman,
The, 61, 127–135, 136
IPC Films, 120

Jampolis, Neil Peter, 169
Johnson, Arte, 49, 50, 59

Keyes, Paul, 59

Landis, John, 128–129
Lasser, Louise, 85
Late Show, The, 89–90, 91,
191, 196
"Laugh-In." See "Rowan and
Martin's Laugh-In"
Libertini, Richard, 144
Lily (ABC), 68–69, 72
Lily (CBS), 67–68
Lily for President?, 149–150
Lily: Sold Out, 70, 145–149
Lily Tomlin, 38, 170–175
Lily Tomlin Show, The, 65–67,
70
Lily Tomlin: On Stage,
103–104
Lohmann, Paul, 84
Lynn, Loretta, 85

McCormick, Kevin, 109–110,
116
Martin, Dick, 50
Martin, Steve, 136, 138, 142,
143
"Merv Griffin Show, The,"
37–38, 41
Michaels, Lorne, 9–10, 66, 68,
70, 74, 75, 86
Midler, Bette, 177, 178–179,
180, 181–182, 183, 184,
185, 186, 187, 188,
193–194
Miller, Marilyn, 74
Modern Scream, 72–74
Moment by Moment, 61,
107–117, 119, 121, 125,
156
Munderloh, Otts, 169
Murphy, Michael, 78
"Music Show, The," 38–39, 41

Nashville, 77–85, 87, 91, 105,
196
NBC, 60, 85
New York Film Critics Award,
80
9 to 5, 119–127

Owens, Gary, 50

Parton, Dolly, 119, 121–122, 123
Paul Simon Special, The,
86–87
People, 85–86
Peyser, Michael, 179–180
Photo Finish, 37
Pierson, Dori, 178, 179
Pinn, Irene M., 32
Polydor, 57, 64
Pryor, Richard, 65, 66, 67, 68,
105, 196

Reiner, Carl, 136–137, 138, 141, 144–145
Resnick, Patricia, 122
Robinson, Phil, 136–137, 138
Rowan, Dan, 50
"Rowan and Martin's Laugh-In," 2, 7, 27, 31, 41–54, 55, 59, 63, 105, 127
Rubel, Marc, 178, 179
Rusk, Jim, 33

Sargent, Herb, 68
"Saturday Night Live," 74–75
Schlatter, George, 7, 41, 42, 43, 47, 48, 54, 59
Schumacher, Joel, 127, 129
Search for Signs of Intelligent Life in the Universe, The, 3, 28, 61–62, 103, 150, 153–175, 185, 192
Simon, Paul, 86
Smith, Madolyn, 144
Swannack, Cheryl, 172

Tewkesbury, Joan, 78
This Is a Recording, 57, 58
Time cover story, 105
"Today," 72
Tomlin, Guy (father), 12, 13, 55
Tomlin, Lillie Mae Ford (mother), 11, 13
Tomlin, Lily
  adolescence of, 17–20
  birth of, 11–12
  as cheerleader, 17, 18
  childhood of, 7, 11–17
  energy of, 17, 34, 35, 97, 168, 191
  future projects of, 188–189
  as perfectionist, 8, 28, 91, 180, 191, 192, 193, 194
  performing in coffeehouses,

  cabarets, and nightclubs, 26–28, 29, 30–31, 32, 36–37, 57–58, 94, 147, 197
  performing in college, 20–23
  physical appearance of, 2, 9, 17, 18
  as private person, 175, 195
  and sexuality, 62–63
  social and political viewpoints of, 9, 70, 71–72
  at Wayne State University, 20–23
  as workaholic, 8, 118, 195
Tomlin, Mary Jean. See Tomlin, Lily
Tomlin, Richard (brother), 13, 118
"Tonight Show, The," 63
Tony Award, 103, 159
tours, 70, 95, 103, 151, 169, 189
Travolta, John, 107, 109, 110, 111, 113, 115

Universal, 116, 129
Unstabled, The, 26, 27
Upstairs at the Downstairs, 36–37

Wagner, Jane, 5–6, 60–62, 64, 67, 68, 85, 93, 94, 98, 104, 107, 108, 109, 115, 128, 131, 149, 153, 154, 155–156, 157, 158, 160, 161, 162, 167–168, 179, 180
Walters, Barbara, 72
Ward, Fred, 184
work shows, 153–155, 170, 172
Worley, Jo Anne, 48
writing, 3, 30, 37, 57,61, 68, 79, 86, 93, 94, 128